Also by J.R.T. Wood:
The Public Career of John, Second Earl of Stair, to 1720
The Welensky Papers: A History of the Federation of Rhodesia and Nyasaland, 1953–1963 (1983)
The War Diaries of André Dennison (1989)
So Far and No Further! Rhodesia's Bid for Independence During the Retreat from Empire 1959-1965 (2005)
A Matter of Weeks Rather than Months: Sanctions and Abortive Settlements: 1965–1969 (2008)
Counter-Strike from the Sky: The Rhodesian All-Arms Fireforce in the War in the Bush, 1974–1980 (2009)

Co-published in 2011 by:

Helion & Company Limited
26 Willow Road
Solihull
West Midlands
B91 1UE
England
Tel. 0121 705 3393
Fax 0121 711 4075
email: info@helion.co.uk
website: www.helion.co.uk

and

30° South Publishers (Pty) Ltd.
16 Ivy Road
Pinetown 3610
South Africa
email: office@30degreessouth.co.za
website: www.30degreessouth.co.za

Text © Richard Wood, 2011
Photographs © as individually credited
Maps © Richard Wood, 2011

Designed & typeset by 30° South Publishers (Pty) Ltd., South Africa
Cover design by 30° South Publishers (Pty) Ltd., South Africa
Printed by Henry Ling Limited, Dorchester, Dorset, UK
ISBN 978-1-907677-36-6

British Library Cataloguing-in-Publication Data
A catalogue record for this book is available from the British Library

All rights reserved. No part of this publication may be reproduced, stored, manipulated in any retrieval system, or transmitted in any mechanical, electronic form or by any other means, without the prior written authority of the publishers, except for short extracts in media reviews. Any person who engages in any unauthorized activity in relation to this publication shall be liable to criminal prosecution and claims for civil and criminal damages.

Front cover: Rhodesian Light Infantry paras emplaning to an Alouette III helicopter (photo courtesy of Dennis Croukamp).

CONTENTS

Glossary	2
Chapter 1: The Background	2
Chapter 2: The Rhodesian Security Forces	7
Chapter 3: The African Nationalist Revolt, the *Chimurenga*, and the Rhodesian Response	10
Chapter 4: The Plan	23
Chapter 5: The Go-Ahead for Operation *Dingo*	28
Chapter 6: The Briefing for the Attack on New Farm, Chimoio	29
Chapter 7: Zulu 1: The Attack on New Farm, Chimoio, 23–24 November 1977	34
0741–0815hrs (H-4 to H+45 minutes)	34
0830–0930hrs	41
0930–1100hrs	43
1100–1212hrs	43
1219–1230hrs	44
1230–1400hrs	46
1400–1730hrs	47
1730–0530hrs	48
0530–1900hrs	48
Chapter 8: Ian Smith's Declaration, 24 November 1977	50
Chapter 9: The Preparation for the Attack on Tembué	51
Chapter 10: Zulu 2: The Attack on Tembué, 26–27 November 1977	52
0800hrs (H-Hour)	53
0804–0810hrs	54
0810–0917hrs	54
0924–1015hrs	55
1016–1145hrs	56
1145–1245hrs	57
1245–1354hrs	59
1354–1449hrs	59
1449–0515hrs	59
0515–1310hrs	60
Chapter 11: The Third Blow: Operation *Virile*, 27–30 November 1977	61
Chapter 12: The Consequences	62

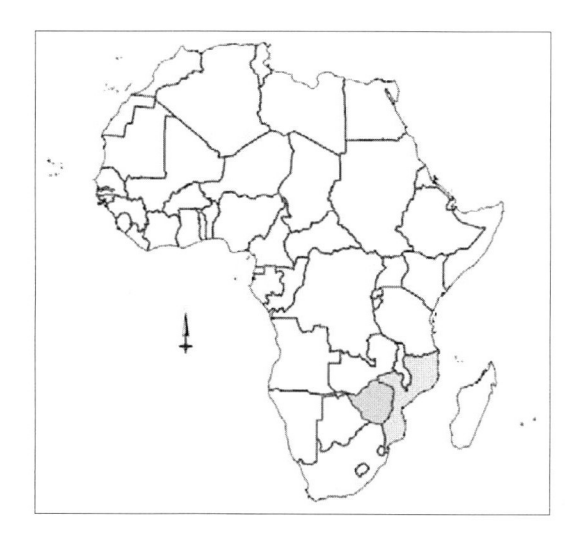

GLOSSARY

ANFO	ammonium nitrate and fuel oil explosive mixture	PATU	Police Anti-Terrorist Unit
BSAP	British South Africa Police	ter/terr	terrorist (slang)
ComOps	Combined Operations Headquarters	RAF	Royal Air Force
CT	Communist terrorist	RAR	Rhodesian African Rifles
FAF	forward airfield	RhAF	Rhodesian Air Force
FN	*Fabrique Nationale*, Belgian arms manufacturer	RIC	Rhodesian Intelligence Corps
FPLM	*Forças Populares para o Libertaçáo de Moçambique*	RLI	Rhodesian Light Infantry
Frantan	frangible tank napalm bomb	RR	Rhodesia Regiment
FRELIMO	*Frente de Libertaçao de Moçambique*	RRAF	Royal Rhodesian Air Force
G-Car	Alouette III helicopter troop-carrier	RRR	Royal Rhodesia Regiment
Golf bomb	460kg Rhodesian-made pressure bomb	SAS	Special Air Service
gomo	hill (Shona)	SB	Special Branch
JOC	Joint Operational Centre	TTL	Tribal Trust Land
K-Car	Alouette III helicopter gunship	UANC	United African National Council
MAG	*Mitrailleuse d'Appui General*, 7.62 x 51mm general-purpose machine gun	ZANLA	Zimbabwe African National Liberation Army
MID	Military Intelligence Directorate	ZANU	Zimbabwe African National Union
Mini-Golf	small version of the Golf bomb	ZAPU	Zimbabwe African People's Union
NCO	non-commissioned officer	ZIPRA	Zimbabwe People's Liberation Army

CHAPTER ONE:
THE BACKGROUND

With devastating effect, Operation *Dingo* achieved one of its purposes. Its consecutive attacks on two major bases damaged the morale and set back the war effort of Robert Mugabe's Zimbabwe African National Liberation Army (ZANLA). Exploiting Rhodesian experience with airborne joint operations, *Dingo* also set the template for further raids against other ZANLA bases in Mozambique and those in Zambia of the Zimbabwe People's Revolutionary Army (ZPRA) of Mugabe's rival, Joshua Nkomo. Never again would the insurgents be caught so unawares as they were on *Dingo*.

Dingo was, however, not just a punitive raid. It belonged to the Dien Bien Phu stable of operations which aimed to weaken an opponent politically. For this reason, Ian Smith, Rhodesia's Prime Minister, finally sanctioned *Dingo* in mid-November 1977.

Dingo was not the first or the last time the Rhodesians used this ploy. They had already done so in October 1976 after B.J. Vorster, the South African Prime Minister, with the help of Henry Kissinger, the United States Secretary of State, had forced Smith to seek a settlement with Nkomo and Mugabe at Geneva. Given that ZANLA was more threatening than ZPRA, the Rhodesian security forces had then launched Operation *Mardon*, comprising simultaneous ground attacks against ZANLA bases close to the Mozambican border. They did so just as the doomed-to-be-abortive Geneva Conference opened with all protagonists present including Mugabe and Nkomo. After *Dingo*, the Rhodesians repeated the strategy in September 1979 when the parties to the Rhodesian dispute met at Lancaster House in London under the chairmanship of Lord Carrington, the British Foreign Secretary. With significant South African help, Operation *Uric/Bootlace* launched a series of air and airborne attacks designed to cut ZANLA's lines of communication and to destroy its bases and war matériel in Mozambique's Gaza Province. Its political purpose was again to weaken Mugabe's hand and to persuade his Mozambican host, President Samora Machel, to withdraw his support. An outcome was that, after the destruction of the bridges across the Limpopo River, Machel forced Mugabe to stay at Lancaster House and accept what the British offered. In October 1979, the Rhodesians repeated the prescription for Nkomo and his host, Kenneth Kaunda, the Zambian president. Operation *Dice* destroyed Zambian bridges and prompted Kaunda to induce Nkomo to settle. The Rhodesian security forces had played their part but their political master, Bishop Abel Muzorewa, Zimbabwe-Rhodesia's first and only Prime Minister, ignored the advice of the more experienced. He placed his trust in the British and their plan, thereby condemning Zimbabwe to what would follow.

All these operations occurred in the final phase of the African nationalist insurgency from which modern Zimbabwe emerged.

CHAPTER ONE: THE BACKGROUND

Robert Mugabe.

Joshua Nkomo.

Bishop Abel Muzorewa.

Ian Smith.

The insurgency had its roots in African resistance to the last surge of the European 'Scramble for Africa' in the second half of the nineteenth century. The insurgency was revived by Britain's post-1945 abandonment of her empire and then by the Eastern Bloc's Cold War strategy of sponsoring 'liberation struggles' in Europe's colonies as proxy wars to weaken the West. A result was the worldwide flooding of volatile areas with Soviet-designed AK assault rifles and similar weapons, a move which, in particular, has cursed Africa ever since.

A number of nationalist insurgencies in Palestine, Malaya, Cyprus and Kenya, plus American pressure, the Suez Crisis, the parlous state of Britain's post-war finances, the burden of the Cold War and a desire to enter the European Economic Union convinced the British to ditch their empire. They did so just as the French and Belgians reached the same conclusion. Having lost Indo-China in 1954 and after a stiff rearguard counter-insurgency action in Algeria, General de Gaulle, the French president, announced in September 1959 a withdrawal from most overseas possessions. Algeria achieved full independence in 1962. De Gaulle immediately advanced all French West African colonies peacefully to independence and cunningly retained an enduring influence over them. The Belgians, by contrast, by a sudden withdrawal, precipitated chaos in the Congo, Ruanda and Burundi. This degenerated into violence including attacks on local whites which had a profound effect on the white Rhodesian psyche.

The British, despite not possessing a written constitution of their own, wrote some 600 interim and final constitutions as they marched their colonies rapidly to independence. In the mid-1950s, the British had begun their withdrawal from West Africa and planned that their East and Central African colonies would achieve independence in the 1970s to allow time for the necessary training. In 1959, however, Harold Macmillan, the British Prime Minister, brought the process forward by more than ten years. This meant that independence was granted to countries which lacked the skills of government. Power was handed to demagogues who immediately created one-party states. Pretending that these were acceptable variants of democracies, they were immediately blessed and indeed courted by the British who were anxious to preserve the Commonwealth and their economic influence and investments.

Frelimo officers inspecting damage at Barragem bridge.
Photo: Noticias

It was easy for Britain to rid herself of colonies and protectorates where executive governors had ruled under the aegis of the Colonial Office. The thorn in their side was Southern Rhodesia because she was self-governing and her electorate was in no mood to succumb, even when the British demolished the promising Federation of Rhodesia and Nyasaland in 1963 by granting independence to Northern Rhodesia (later Zambia) and Nyasaland (Malawi).

This spirit of independence was imbued in the manner of the founding of Rhodesia. It was not a product of British imperial expansion. Instead the initiative came from Cecil Rhodes, the mining magnate, founder of the Cape fruit industry and a Cape politician. In 1888, seeking further gold reefs north of the Transvaal Republic, Rhodes secured a mining concession from the Ndebele King, Lobengula. The concession covered Mashonaland, the area to the northeast of Lobengula's fiefdom. In an attempt to divide and rule, Lobengula then gave Rhodes's German rival, Eduard Lippert, the right to acquire and exploit land. Prompted by this German interest in the area but not wanting any further administrative responsibilities, the British Government granted Rhodes a Royal Charter to exploit the territories north of the Limpopo and south of the Belgian Congo.

Empowered by this, Rhodes formed the British South Africa Company (BSAC) and dispatched a small force of pioneers and police to take possession of Mashonaland in September 1890. By then Rhodes was Prime Minister of the Cape and his new possession would adopt the Cape's Roman-Dutch law and recruit

Cecil John Rhodes.　　Lobengula.

1890 Tuli River crossing, BSAC pioneer column.

its settlers from there. To secure the right to possess land in 1891, Rhodes bought the Lippert concession. The right of ownership of land by immigrants became the main cause of friction, leading to the insurgency. In the 1890s, however, with some 400,000 indigenous inhabitants occupying 390,757 square kilometres (two fifths larger than the United Kingdom), Rhodesia seemed empty with more than enough land for everyone—as is still the case. Rhodesia (a name adopted in 1895) became embroiled in war in 1893 when the Ndebele contested the interference by the BSAC in their traditional practice of raiding their Shona-speaking neighbours. The short Matabele War and the seizure of Matabeleland were followed by the Ndebele and Shona uprisings in 1896. Again the rebellions were suppressed with some British help. The larger Shona uprising, the *Chimurenga*—or war of liberation—took longer to subdue.

Never happy with the rule by a commercial company, particularly after the BSAC-sponsored Jameson Raid in 1896 had embarrassed it, the British Government increased its powers of surveillance of company activity, stripped it of its control of Northern Rhodesia and gave the population a legislative voice on a theoretically non-racial basis as the qualified franchise was based on income or the value of property and not on race.

Unable to make a profit out of its Rhodesian holdings and given pressure from the increasingly impatient white electorate, the BSAC held a referendum in 1922 offering, at the behest of the British Government, incorporation in the Union of South Africa or self-government. With the Boer War (in which Rhodesians had fought for Britain) still a raw memory and for a host of other reasons, the electorate chose self-government, believing it to be a step to dominion status. The colonial secretary, Winston Churchill, conferred self-governing status on Southern Rhodesia with the right of defence, a prime minister, a cabinet government and a legislative assembly or parliament. Britain retained certain powers over African affairs, including a veto to protect the newly designated African reserves. As before, the vote was given to adults of any race provided they were British subjects and had a minimum level of income or a matching value of property. The non-racial franchise would endure until 1961 when the British forced the Rhodesians to introduce a racial one.

A highly stylized and unrealistic portrayal of the raider's last stand at Doornkop.
Photo: Jameson's Raid

CHAPTER ONE: THE BACKGROUND

A ageing Rhodesian Air Force fleet. Seen here is a formation of four Canberra bombers and six Hawker Hunters.
Photo: Peter Petter-Bowyer / Winds of Destruction

In 1924, therefore, Rhodesia ranked with New Zealand before the latter was granted dominion status. Southern Rhodesia not only came under the aegis of the Dominions Office but also attended all Commonwealth Prime Ministers' conferences until 1964 when the British suddenly withdrew the invitation for fear of offending the new African members like Kenneth Kaunda of Zambia.

The Rhodesian whites were independently minded. They had to be, living in a raw new country where self-reliance was paramount. Even so they remained fiercely loyal to king and country, fighting in the Boer, First and Second World Wars. Not wanting to replicate the 'poor white' problem in South Africa, Southern Rhodesia imposed monetary and income qualifications on would-be immigrants because the African population supplied the country's unskilled labour wants. This meant when white Rhodesians went to war in 1939, being the first of the Commonwealth to declare war, they fought more in leadership positions than in the ranks and in most theatres of the war. After 1945, alone among the British colonies as opposed to the dominions, the Rhodesians would meet their Commonwealth obligations by sending their regular troops to serve in the Canal Zone, Malaya and Aden while the Royal Rhodesian Air Force flew in support of the Royal Air Force in the Middle East.

The Rhodesians, in the person of their Prime Minister, Sir Godfrey Huggins (later Lord Malvern), were aware the British Labour Party had proclaimed in 1943 their intention to disband the British Empire. This sharpened a movement toward amalgamating Northern and Southern Rhodesia under the Southern Rhodesian 1923 constitution and with Salisbury (now Harare) as the capital. Pressure on the new British Labour Government from Huggins and from the leader of the unofficial members in the Northern Rhodesian Legislative Council, the aggressive and able Roy Welensky, resulted in a compromise which bucked the decolonization trend. In 1948 the British Labour Government sanctioned the formation of a federation of the two Rhodesias but added in the impoverished protectorate of Nyasaland.

The Federation had only ten years to live because the British had retained control, through executive governors, of African affairs in Northern Rhodesia and Nyasaland while allowing the Federal Government finance, defence, transport and the like. So when the cry for independence coupled with violent unrest came from the new African nationalists—Harry Nkumbula, Kenneth Kaunda and Hastings Banda— the British conceded it even though the nationalists had barely sat in a parliament and it meant the break-up of the Federation.

The most developed of the three federal territories, Southern Rhodesia, however, was emphatically denied independence until she implemented majority rule. This was despite the dropping of colour bars and the acceptance in 1961 by the electorate of the new constitution designed to bring about a political evolution as the African majority qualified for the franchise and won seats.

In the 1960s the British demand was that advancement to majority rule should take no more than the life of a parliament. To the Rhodesian electorate this was madness as the Africans were clearly not ready for government and such a transfer could risk a descent into Congo-like chaos. Stalemate ensued. To the impatient African nationalists, seeing power being handed to their fellow nationalists in Tanganyika, Kenya, Uganda, Somalia and elsewhere, the prospect of a slow evolution was unendurable.

For a long time an urban phenomenon, because the rural people remained under the thrall of their chiefs, the small African nationalist movement challenged the status quo in Southern Rhodesia. They did so with the support of a handful of sympathetic liberal whites including the ex-Prime Minister, Garfield Todd but not of the bulk of the Rhodesian whites.

As the African nationalists' frustrated challenge became more violent, with the petrol bomb as a preferred method of intimidation, so the Southern Rhodesian Government toughened its security laws and strengthened the BSAP. As defence was its responsibility and, prompted by the Congo crisis in 1960, the Federal Government likewise raised new all-white units and re-equipped the RRAF with new aircraft. In the event, as early as 1956, sensing the trend in Africa, the Federal Army and RRAF had devoted training time to an internal security role.

The Rhodesian Government's response to the African nationalists was to ban their organizations and to detain their leaders. Increasingly the African nationalists looked externally for assistance, finding a sympathetic ear in the Communist Bloc. Soon the Comintern in Moscow was funding, training and arming the nationalists after the Zimbabwe African People's Union (ZAPU), led by Nkomo, had decided in 1961 to initiate an 'Armed Struggle' on the Marxist-Leninist model. Umkhonto we Sizwe, the armed wing of the South African African National Congress (SAANC) and ZAPU's ally, did likewise and also found a willing patron in the Soviet Union. ZAPU, however, endured a schism in 1963 when, impatient with slow progress by Nkomo, a mainly Shona-speaking faction led by the Reverend Ndabaningi Sithole broke away to form the Zimbabwe African National Union (ZANU). Later, Robert Mugabe would oust Sithole in a leadership coup in 1974. ZANU would capitalize on the Sino-Soviet split of 1961. Keen to rival the Soviet influence in Africa as well as to subvert western interests, the Chinese Communists, the North Koreans and dissident Communist states like Yugoslavia readily supplied ZANU with training and weapons.

In 1964–1965 the 'Armed Struggle' was as yet still-born as the Rhodesians, aided by penetration of nationalist ranks, had good notice of the early moves and uncovered the perpetrators of sabotage of railway lines and the like. At that moment, with the British Government stonewalling Ian Smith, the new Rhodesian Prime Minister, Smith declared Rhodesia unilaterally independent (UDI). Outraged, the British Prime Minister, Harold Wilson, responded by declaring UDI and Smith's government illegal and by persuading the United Nations to follow suit and to apply economic sanctions. Sanctions, of course, made life in Rhodesia difficult and the replacement of military aircraft in particular in some cases impossible.

UDI put Rhodesia beyond the pale. Without any prospect of diplomatic recognition, Smith was forced to seek a settlement with the British. Whatever Smith said in public, he understood that the Rhodesian white population, never more than four per cent of the population, could not dominate forever. He sought, however, a political and social evolution, something which would never satisfy the impatient African nationalists who saw their counterparts in the British crown colonies already enjoying power.

Smith met Harold Wilson on the Royal navy warships, HMS *Tiger* and *Fearless*, in 1966 and 1968, but could not accept the terms offered him, mostly because Wilson was determined that Rhodesia would be governed directly by Whitehall for a short period before independence was granted. As Rhodesia had never been governed by Whitehall, this was unacceptable to Smith and his Rhodesian Front party and most of the Rhodesian electorate.

The incoming Conservative Government of Edward Heath had the wit to drop that idea and Smith accepted the deal offered by Sir Alec Douglas-Home in 1971. He had, however, earlier made the mistake of agreeing that any settlement had to be found to be acceptable to *all* the inhabitants of Rhodesia. In essence, this gave the African population as a whole a veto. Consequently, African nationalists, led by Bishop Abel Muzorewa, seized the chance to ensure, by every means on hand, the rejection of the Home–Smith agreement by the six per cent sample poll of the views of the population assessed by the British-appointed Pearce Commission.

The British withdrew the settlement proposals and the returning British Prime Minister, Harold Wilson, and his foreign minister, James Callaghan, refused to offer anything more. They did so against the background of the global recession fuelled by the OPEC oil embargo, a consequence of the Yon Kippur War of 1973. Dependent on exports and oil imports, both of which had to evade UN sanctions, Rhodesia was hard hit.

Then the Portuguese coup of 1974 brought the veteran insurgent, Samora Machel, to power in Mozambique and opened Rhodesia's entire eastern flank to ZANLA while closing her access to her nearest ports. Thenceforth Rhodesia not only had the additional cost of long rail-freight journeys to the South African ports but was also totally reliant on the political whims of a South African Government when it was vainly seeking to survive by reaching an accommodation with independent African states. Pressed to settle by B.J. Vorster, the South African Prime Minister, Ian Smith had no choice but to attempt to do so, firstly with Bishop Abel Muzorewa and then with Nkomo. All the negotiations in 1973–1976 were abortive. Muzorewa signed one agreement and then reneged. Nkomo could not be pinned down and Smith could not accept immediate majority rule and survive politically.

By early 1976, James Callaghan, upon succeeding Harold Wilson as British Prime Minister, conspired with Henry Kissinger, the US Secretary of State, and Vorster to force Smith to seek a settlement on the basis of majority rule within two years. Consequently the British convened a conference of all parties in Geneva in October 1976.

The British government and its chairman, Ivor Richard, however, proved unable and, indeed unwilling, to adhere to what Smith had agreed with Kissinger and to resist the nationalist demands for immediate majority rule. The Rhodesians withdrew only to be faced by another unacceptable plan proposed in 1977 by David Owen (now Lord Owen), the British Foreign Secretary, and Cyrus Vance, the new US Secretary of State.

Ian Smith turned his back on them in favour again of settling with internal African nationalists, Bishop Muzorewa and the Reverend Sithole and the tribal leader, Chief Jeremiah Chirau, all of whom were by then avowed enemies of Nkomo and Mugabe. By late 1977, the negotiations had made sufficient progress for Smith to be ready to announce that a majority-rule government would be a reality in 1978. Before making that announcement, Smith wanted to use Operation *Dingo* to silence Mugabe or at least diminish his influence.

CHAPTER TWO:
THE RHODESIAN SECURITY FORCES

Murray's BSAP contingent, sent to German East Africa (now Tanzania) in 1915.
Photo: Blue and Old Gold

Sergeant Frederick Charles Booth VC DCM, pictured in 1918 after winning his Victoria Cross. He was attached to the Rhodesia Native Regiment on its formation in 1916 and accompanied it to East Africa.
Photo: Blue and Old Gold

Faced with any challenge, governments ultimately act or abdicate. The means with which to face the challenge of adoption of the 'Armed Struggle' in 1961 already existed in Rhodesia. The British South Africa Company had bequeathed to Southern Rhodesia the British South Africa Police (BSAP), the successor to the BSAC Police, the 500 men who had guarded the Pioneer Column. As the only regular force before 1927, the BSAP was responsible for the defence of Southern Rhodesia as well as maintaining law and order. Local volunteer forces supplemented its efforts in the turbulent first years. The volunteers became the Rhodesia Regiment and saw service in East Africa in the First World War along with the short-lived Rhodesian Native Regiment. The BSAP supported both regiments with men and training. Some members of the Rhodesia Regiment found themselves serving on the Western Front incorporated into the ranks of the South African Army and paid a heavy price.

The BSAP retained its role as the first line of defence until the 1950s, parading as the 'Right of the Line'. Although initially conceived as a mounted gendarmerie and always calling itself 'The Regiment', the BSAP adhered to the British tradition of policemen only being armed in times of emergency. The exception was its small, and at first largely ceremonial, paramilitary Support Unit. Southern Rhodesia, however, never just relied for defence on a gendarmerie. Having been conferred the right of defence by the 1923 Constitution, in 1927 Southern Rhodesia instituted compulsory part-time (territorial) military service for young white males in the hitherto voluntary Rhodesia Regiment. The regiment comprised the First Battalion in Salisbury and the Second in Bulawayo, a company in Gwelo (now Gweru) and rural rifle platoons. A small Permanent Staff Corps was raised to train them at yearly camps and weekend parades with the emphasis on the basics of conventional or classical warfare. The first recruits for the Staff Corps were drawn from the ranks of the BSAP, many of whom had military experience.

The growing European crisis after 1936 led to the formation of an air wing, the fledging Southern Rhodesia Air Force (SRAF), flying a handful of obsolete biplanes.

In 1939, Southern Rhodesia was the first of the British Empire to follow Britain's lead in declaring war on Germany, dispatching SRAF to reinforce the British forces in East Africa and calling up all white men of military age. The Rhodesia Regiment was retained for home defence and served by part-time personnel who were over military age or in reserved civilian jobs. Because of the heavy casualties suffered in the First World War, Rhodesia decided to disperse her personnel among British services and then in 1941 formed an anti-tank gun unit, the Southern Rhodesia Armoured Car Regiment, a medical unit and a patrol of the Long Range Desert Group. Because of the calibre of the Rhodesian servicemen and women, many served as officers and NCOs. The Royal West Africa Frontier Force, for example, had a Rhodesian leadership corps. Rhodesians were to be found in all theatres of the war on land, sea and in the air. The only regular regiment formed was the white-officered Rhodesian African Rifles (RAR), which served with the 44 East African Division in Burma. The SRAF was absorbed into the RAF as No. 237 Squadron in which Flight Lieutenant Ian Smith, for one, served with distinction. Other Rhodesians were drafted into No. 44 bomber and No. 266 fighter squadrons. In all some 10,000 young white Rhodesians fought.

1RAR troops crossing a ravine on a temporary bridge in the Arakan.
Photo: Masodja

Askaris of 1RAR resting in a dugout.
Photo: Masodja

Lt-Gen Peter Walls.

Selous Scout Ron Reid-Daly.

The SRAF was revived shortly after the Second World War and the RAR was retained, as was compulsory territorial training for the Rhodesia Regiment, and the reformed Rhodesian Armoured Car Regiment, Rhodesian Artillery and Corps of Engineers and Signals. The SRAF flew Harvard trainers and Spitfire Mk XIIs and later Vampire Mk IX jet fighter-bombers and Percival Provost Mk 52 trainers after a generous donation by the Northern Rhodesian Government. In 1951, 100 volunteers, commanded by Major Peter Walls, formed C Squadron of the Malayan Scouts. Their service in Malaya gave Rhodesia a cadre of men experienced in counter-insurgency, among them the future commander of the Selous Scouts, Ronald Reid-Daly. Raised by Brigadier 'Mad' Mike Calvert, the Malayan Scouts became the British 22 SAS Regiment in 1952.

After 1953 when defence became its responsibility, the Federal Government created an African, white-officered regular infantry brigade with the RAR joining the Northern Rhodesia Regiment and the First and Second King's African Rifles of Nyasaland. The brigade was backed by an expanded Rhodesia Regiment to absorb non-African national servicemen, conscripted for four and a half months of initial training at the regimental depot, the Llewellin Barracks, near Bulawayo, by the Staff Corps. A leadership-training establishment, the School of Infantry, was established at Gwelo. The Rhodesia Regiment had three active and seven reserve battalions. The trained men of the active battalions had an obligation of three years' territorial service which included weekend parades and annual camps. The reservists had a diminished service obligation.

Financial restraints in 1956 saw the disbanding of the Rhodesian Armoured Cars and engineers. The artillery was reduced to the Governor-General's Saluting Troop. In 1957, however, the problem of the Federal Army's logistics led to the formation of the Rhodesian Army Services Corps. As already mentioned, the regular Federal Army units served abroad in the Suez Canal Zone, Malaya and Aden. The RRAF flew with the RAF in Cyprus and Aden again gaining vital experience. To meet these obligations, the RRAF acquired the long-range medium bomber, the Canberra B2 and the Hawker Hunter Mk IX fighter.

Stirrings of unrest in the ranks of the African nationalists in all three of the Federal territories, prompted the Federal Government in 1956 to implement internal security training even though this remained the prime responsibility of the police forces of the three territories.

The 1959 Nyasaland Emergency.
Photo: Rob Southey

CHAPTER TWO: THE RHODESIAN SECURITY FORCES

Early days of the Rhodesian Light Infantry (RLI)—classical war training.
Photo: The Saints

In the early months of 1959, Dr Hastings Banda and his Nyasaland African National Congress (later the Malawi Congress Party) threatened to seize power in Nyasaland. The Federal Army and riot units from the BSAP, the Northern Rhodesian and Tanganyika Police reinforced the under-strength Nyasaland Police and order was restored by April 1959.

The deployment of 6,000 regular and territorial troops in Nyasaland exposed several weaknesses and technical wants in the Federal Army. One was the need for quick reaction in territories with few roads which showed the need for helicopters and paratroops. The lack of radio communications was another.

The dramatically changing political African landscape in 1960 as a consequence of the abandonment of empire, with the Congolese Army mutinying and that country descending into bloody chaos, impelled the Federal Government in February 1961 to form the exclusively white infantry battalion, the Rhodesian Light Infantry (1RLI) and an armoured car squadron, the Selous Scouts (not to be confused with the later, eponymous and more famous counter-insurgency unit). The cost of defence, however, led to the questioning of the Federal commitment of an infantry brigade to the defence of the Commonwealth. In response, the Chief of Imperial General Staff, Admiral Lord Mountbatten, proposed instead the revival of Rhodesia's C Squadron of the British 22 SAS Regiment. C Squadron would serve in Aden. The formation of the SAS met the Federal Army's airborne requirement which the Federal Government bolstered with the purchase of French Alouette III jet-engined helicopters. Although small, the Alouette was versatile and, most importantly, capable of flying in the hot climate and the high altitude of Rhodesia, conditions which challenged other contemporary makes of helicopters. Despite its limited carrying capacity and short range, the Rhodesians would exploit the versatility of the tough little helicopter to the maximum. They dealt with the problem of range by depositing fuel at rural police stations and district offices around the country.

The demise of Federation on 31 January 1963, however, and the refusal of independence to Rhodesia led Africa's newly independent countries like Tanganyika to deny the RRAF overflying rights and thereby ended Rhodesia's commitment to the Commonwealth before UDI in 1965.

The loss of the Federal revenues and British denial of monies owed from the dissolution, coupled with an unofficial Anglo-American arms embargo—part of the pressure being applied on Ian Smith to accept rapid progress of majority rule—meant the Rhodesian armed forces were unable to replace major assets even before, let alone after, Ian Smith had declared UDI. In addition, the independence of Zambia in 1964 robbed the Rhodesia Regiment of the 3rd (active) and the 7th (reserve) battalions. Thus

Prime Minister Ian Smith signs the unilateral declaration of independence on 11 November 1965.
Photo: So Far and No Further!

the Rhodesian services faced an uncertain future in November 1965 with ageing aircraft and equipment. Many servicemen had taken advantage of Federal 'golden-handshakes' (termination of contracts) depleting the RLI and C Squadron SAS as they prepared, with the RAR and the part-timers of the diminished Rhodesia Regiment, to defend Rhodesia and to assist the BSAP to counter African nationalist insurgency. They could, however, take comfort for the moment from the weakness and lack of preparedness of their African nationalist opponents who had not as yet secured significant support among the Rhodesian African population.

CHAPTER THREE:
THE AFRICAN NATIONALIST REVOLT, THE *CHIMURENGA*, AND THE RHODESIAN RESPONSE

Harari Township, Salisbury, 1963. Tear-gar projectiles at the ready, a riot squad prepares for confrontation.
Photo: Blue and Old Gold

Riot police stand firm against a crowd of demonstrators in Mabvuku Township, Salisbury, 1964.
Photo: Blue and Old Gold

Preventive detention, the banning of parties and other counter measures to the urban unrest stirred up by the African nationalists in 1960–1963, had driven the rebels either underground or into exile in Zambia. From the latter, lacking both trained manpower and recruits, ZAPU mounted a sporadic and largely inconsequential sabotage campaign in the period 1962–1965.

ZAPU's rival, ZANU, with Communist China as its inspiration and mentor, sought to mount the 'people's war' on the Maoist prescription. In April 1966, it despatched a small unit of 20 men across the Zambezi River near Chirundu in the hope of sparking an African uprising and to impress ZANU's paymaster, the Organization of African Unity (OAU). To inspire young Africans to join the armed struggle and to frighten the whites into emigrating, Herbert Chitepo, the external leader of ZANU, ordered the team to sabotage the oil pipeline from Beira—even though oil sanctions had already forced its closure—and blow up key road bridges. Although the group split up after entering Rhodesia, they were soon arrested or killed. The deaths of the largest sub-unit of seven at Sinoia (now Chinoyi) on 27 April 1966 was at the hands of the BSAP, supported by the RRAF which deployed an armed helicopter for the first time. This skirmish is now celebrated annually by Zimbabwe as the 'Battle of Chinoyi', the start of the Second *Chimurenga*, or war of liberation. The last and as yet undetected group of the gang murdered Johannes and Johanna Viljoen at Gadzema on 16 May 1966. This incident was characteristic of the first phase of the insurgency.

The first phase, 1966–1972, was dominated by ZAPU which inserted a small team into Rhodesia in July 1966, the first of a further 30 operations, two of which involved ZAPU's ally and fellow Soviet client, the South African African National Congress. The purpose of these parties was also to sponsor a popular revolt and to show the OAU something for its money. Various mistakes by the incoming insurgents allowed the Rhodesian security forces to deal with them in the harsh, dry, thorny and mostly unpopulated Zambezi Valley.

By 1972, although wracked by internal revolts, the ZANU leadership at least realized that, to survive, their cadres had to reach and secure succour from the populated areas along Rhodesia's northern border with Mozambique.

CHAPTER THREE: THE AFRICAN NATIONALIST REVOLT, THE *CHIMURENGA*, AND THE RHODESIAN RESPONSE

'The Battle of Sinoia'
29 April 1966

Labels on map:
- To Sinoia
- To Salisbury
- Open Farm Land
- ZANU group expected to meet the contact here
- Contact entered bush here
- fence
- Major Billy Conn shot two here.
- Lone man under a tree
- Cadre fires at Petter-Bowyer
- Helicopter fires at cadre and kills him here.
- Pilot Officer Becks prevents sweeplines converging here.
- fence

J.R.T. Wood

ZANU's chance came after ZAPU had failed to take up an offer to collaborate with the Mozambican guerrilla movement, the *Frente de Libertação de Moçambique* (FRELIMO). FRELIMO's penetration of the Tete Province opened the vulnerable northeastern border and gave ZANU's infiltrators a population to hide among.

The Rhodesian regular forces, the under-strength RLI and the over-strength regular infantry battalion, 1RAR, were by then overstretched by the task of assisting the BSAP with the control of a thousand or more kilometres of border. This was despite the reinforcement of two or more 100-man companies of the South African Police after the SAANC members had been found during Operation *Nickel* among ZAPU personnel captured in the area of the Wankie Game Reserve in 1967. South African policemen would provide this assistance until 1974 when Vorster withdrew them as part of the pressure on Smith. Not only were the South African Police used to patrol the border but so were the Rhodesia Regiment's national servicemen from its depot at Llewellin Barracks and its territorial and reserve battalions. At first this duty took the place of the annual camps for the territorials and reservists and did not disrupt commerce and industry. It gave the part-time forces valuable experience of practical soldiering in tough conditions.

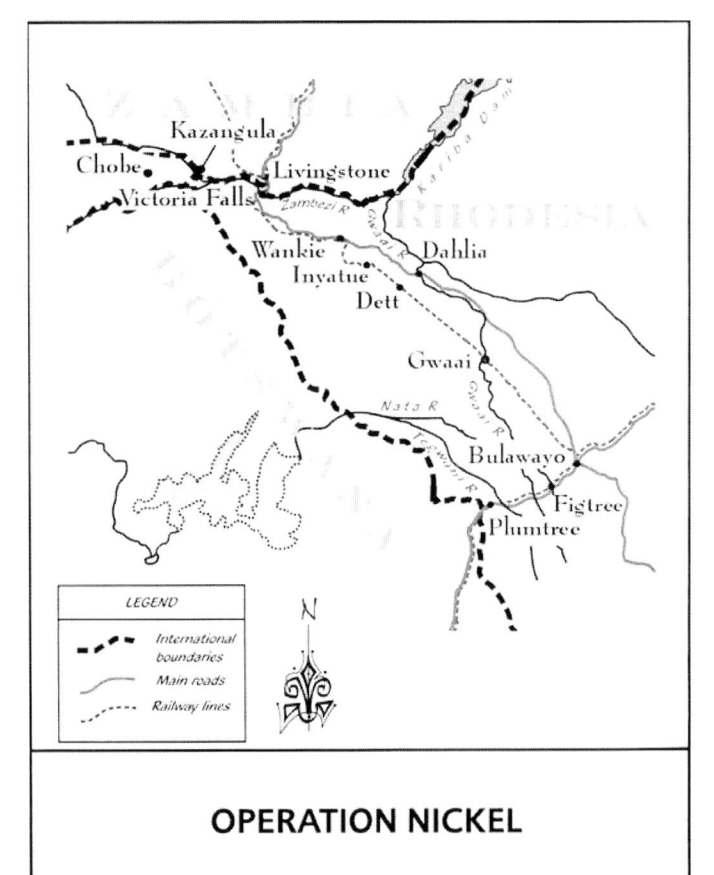

OPERATION NICKEL

Operation *Nickel*.
Photo: The Saints

Operation *Nickel*.
Photo: The Saints

In fact, this first phase readied the Rhodesian security forces for what was to come. Since the advent of Ian Smith in 1964, the army, RRAF and BSAP had been honing their systems. The BSAP had recruited large numbers of white police reservists reinforced by a lesser number of African police reservists. The army was divided into two brigades: 1 Brigade was based in Bulawayo with 1RAR and the Second Battalion of Royal Rhodesia Regiment (2RRR) as its core units, and reinforced by two reserve battalions, 6 and 9RRR. 2 Brigade was in Salisbury with 1RLI and 1RRR as its core units, reinforced by 5 and 8RRR. 10RRR was based in Gwelo and 4RRR in Umtali (now Mutare). C Squadron SAS was designated as Special Forces under command of Army Headquarters in Salisbury. As national service was increased to a six-month period, the RRR depot supplied two independent companies of national servicemen who had completed four and a half months' initial training. These companies were based at Wankie and Kariba. The RRAF recruited territorial members and formed a counter-insurgency squadron, No. 4, to supplement No. 7 (helicopter) Squadron. Intelligence gathering, that crucial element in any counter-insurgency effort, was delegated to a separate bureau, the Central Intelligence Organization, to which the Police Special Branch would be affiliated. The command and control re-organization produced the Security Council, chaired by the prime minister, under which came military and civilian committees tasked with co-ordinating their aspects of the effort. The civil aspects, including psychological action, were the responsibility of the Counter-Insurgency Civil Committee. The military and police matters were dealt with together by the commanders of the three services sitting as the Operations Co-ordinating Committee (OCC). The Joint Planning Staff (JPS), drawn from the three services, provided the OCC's secretariat and a research element. When an incursion was detected, often through information supplied by the African population—a measure of the unpopularity of ZANU and ZAPU—a Joint Operations Centre (JOC) would be established by the OCC at a strategic point to co-ordinate the operation. As the need arose, the RRAF established and staffed forward airfields with 1,000-metre-long runways to allow the use of Douglas Dakota transports.

The JOC system worked well despite an unsteady start when the Commissioner of Police, Frank Barfoot, faced with the first incursion in April 1966, argued that under the Police Act the BSAP alone was charged with the maintenance of order. So, instead of deploying the trained and properly equipped RLI regular troops, the BSAP called up the local police reservists, mostly farmers, and issued them with obsolete .303 Lee-Enfield rifles to face the ZANU infiltrators armed with modern automatic Soviet weapons. The somewhat chaotic yet successful skirmish led to the firm implementation of the JOC system and joint operations thereafter.

The RRAF had also learned lessons in the Sinoia incident and the succeeding operations. One was the need for deflector sights for helicopter machine guns to enable accurate shooting from a moving aircraft. Another was the need to evolve tactics to exploit the maximum potential of the remarkable Alouette. Compatible radios and good, swift communications between air and ground forces were vital. Pilots had to train with the full loads they would carry in combat.

Alouette G-Car gunner technician on his 7.62 MAG, with Collimateur gun sights.
Photo: The Saints

The army also learned hard lessons in the fighting in the Zambezi Valley and honed its tactics. The passenger capacity of the Alouette of only four men resulted in all military units adopting the four-man 'stick'. The stick leader, normally a corporal, and two of his men were armed with Belgian FN FAL (*Fabrique Nationale Fusil Automatique Léger*) rifles and the fourth with an FN MAG (*Mitrailleuse d'Appui General*) general purpose machine gun. Both the FN rifle and the MAG fired the powerful NATO 7.62 x 51mm round, which allowed accurate fire to 600 metres compared with the 300 metres of the Soviet 7.62 x 39mm round of the SKS and AK-47 assault rifles and RPD machine guns used by ZANLA and ZPRA. The corporal would be equipped with a VHF radio, which allowed the stick to operate independently. With all four men also armed with the usual range of grenades, including rifle grenades, both anti-armour and phosphorus, the stick could lay down formidable firepower. The belt-fed MAG, in particular, was a powerful weapon and is still in use on modern battlefields, in Afghanistan for example. Unlike their opponents who tended to rely on automatic fire, the Rhodesian Army laid emphasis on accurate shooting, seeking success with a single round. Accuracy is vital in counter-insurgency operations in order to avoid harming and thereby alienating the innocent.

An RLI trooper slakes his thirst in the searing heat of the Zambezi valley.
Photo: The Saints

Tracking was recognized as an essential skill. In response, led by the ecologist and later politician, Allan Savory, the Tracker Combat Unit was formed to tap the skills of the National Parks personnel, professional hunters and others. In 1969, a tracking school was established at Kariba, staffed by the SAS and under the auspices of the School of Infantry. In the early 1970s, the new Selous Scouts took over the school.

What was not resolved was the lack of manpower. The early operations proved that the regular forces were taxed to the limit by the demand for units both for border control and to deal with infiltrations. An answer was to recruit African soldiers, as there was always an abundance of eager recruits.

National Parks' rangers on patrol at Mana Pools on the Zambezi River.
Photo: The Saints

There was also a need for supporting arms, artillery, armoured cars and more. Given, however, the weight of international sanctions and demands upon a depleted public purse, the Rhodesian Government lacked the funds to support the army's demands, let alone meet all the air force's urgent requirements to replace its ageing aircraft. With all the early incursions being successfully and quickly dealt with, there was also an unfortunate complacency in Rhodesian government circles.

This was shaken when African nationalists within Rhodesia, led by Bishop Abel Muzorewa, organized the rejection of the Home–Smith settlement

RLI follow-up operations in the Zambezi Valley, mid-1960s.
Photo: The Saints

13

agreement in early 1972. It seemed that the urban unrest of the early 1960s had revived itself. Police action quashed it but its potential did not pass unnoticed in Lusaka where the ZANU high command sought new routes into Rhodesia. Cadres of ZANU's military wing, ZANLA, began appearing among groups of FRELIMO insurgents pushing southwest into the Tete Province of Mozambique. The FRELIMO intention was to threaten the new hydroelectric scheme being built by the Portuguese in the Cabora (now Cahora) Bassa gorge on the Zambezi. ZANLA's aim was to subvert the rural African people close to Rhodesia's barely guarded northeastern border and thereby gain a toehold from which to expand ZANU's influence.

Anticipation of this threat had already led to small units of Rhodesian trackers and aircraft being deployed into Tete to assist the Portuguese Army. Because Rhodesia's pariah status ruled out formal international agreements, she concluded a secret defensive co-operation pact with Portugal and South Africa, covering the exchange of intelligence and mutual co-operation. In 1972 the threat from the Tete Province led Rhodesia to mount a couple of cross-border joint operations, one which involved the use of helicopters to move troops tactically on a larger scale than previously—all part of the genesis of the Fireforce and its constant honing of the skills needed to mount operations like *Dingo*.

An attack by ZANLA on the white-owned Altena farm in the Centenary farming area in northeastern Rhodesia on 23 December 1972 signalled the start of the second phase of the insurgency that would last until 1974. What was confirmed was that ZANLA had subverted the local population undetected. Hitherto, the rural Africans had reported the presence of strangers. Now, there was silence. The Rhodesians launched Operation *Hurricane* with its JOC at Centenary. This time there would be no quick result. Indeed, Operation *Hurricane* would endure until the final election in March 1980 handed power to Robert Mugabe and ZANU. With safe havens in Mozambique and applying the Maoist template, ZANLA divided northeastern and later eastern and southeastern Rhodesia into provinces and sectors with the intention of politicizing the rural people, of establishing local committees and infiltration routes. They sought contact men, feeders and porters. They co-opted spirit mediums, cached arms and ammunition and, copying FRELIMO, began to plant landmines to hamper the movement of the security forces. If securing intelligence of the whereabouts and intentions of the insurgents proved difficult,

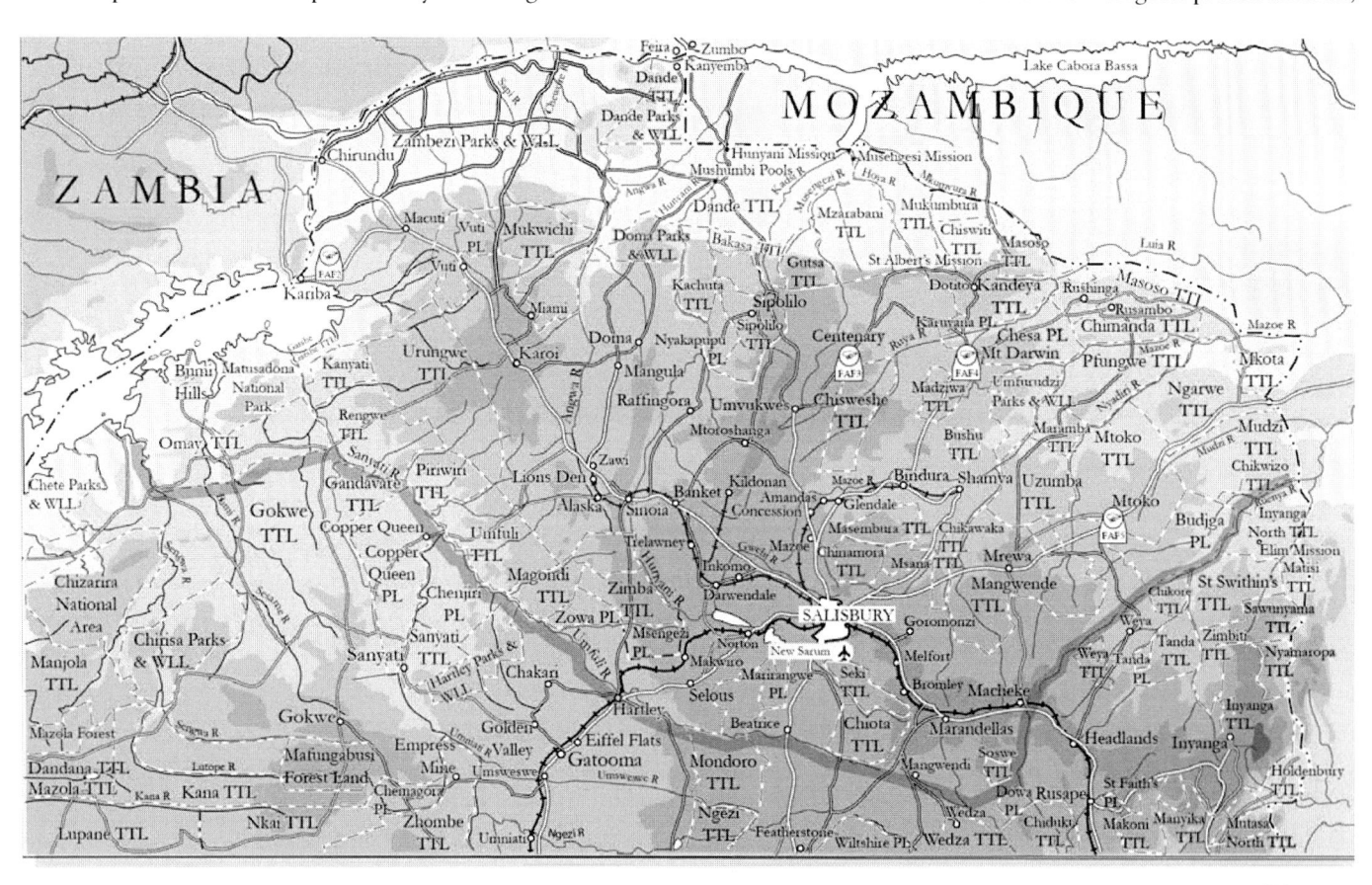

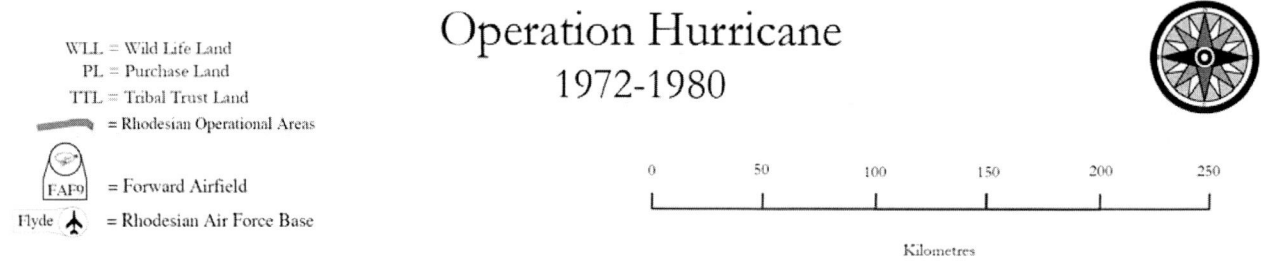

Operation Hurricane
1972–1980

WLL = Wild Life Land
PL = Purchase Land
TTL = Tribal Trust Land
= Rhodesian Operational Areas
FAF9 = Forward Airfield
Hyde = Rhodesian Air Force Base

J.R.T. Wood

ZANLA opened its summer campaign of 1971/2 with attacks on isolated white farms in the Centenary District.
Photo: The Saints

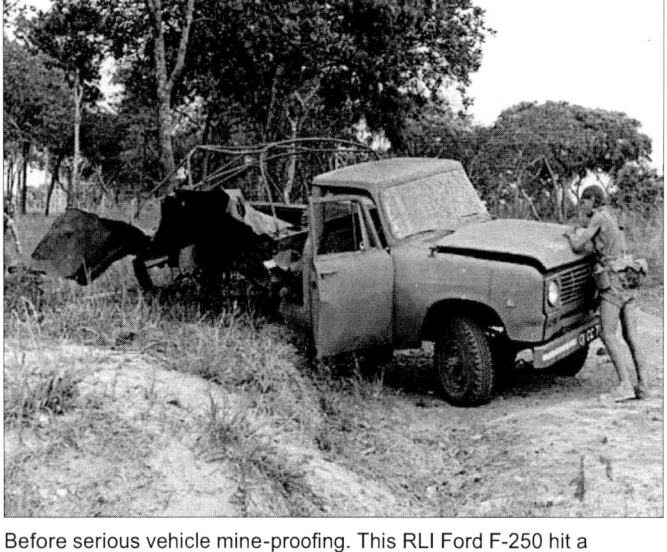

Before serious vehicle mine-proofing. This RLI Ford F-250 hit a landmine and suffered fatalities, Operation Hurricane, 1972
Photo: The Saints

Above and below: Operation Hurricane—Rhodesian Air Force air strikes on enemy positions in the tribal trust lands.
Photo: The Saints

The Pookie mine-detection vehicle, developed in collaboration with the South African CSIR.
Photo: The Saints

the Rhodesian response was robust. Troops scoured the suspected areas. With Portuguese permission, the SAS deployed across the Zambezi in the western end of Tete Province seeking ZANLA's infiltration routes and transit camps and marking them for aerial attack. Any cadres who crossed the river faced interception by the RAR before reaching the Rhodesian border.

Filling tyres with water and protecting truck bodies with rubber conveyor belting and sandbags reduced the toll exacted by the insurgent-laid landmines. This was supplemented by research into mine-protection in collaboration with the South African Council for Scientific and Industrial Research (CSIR) which would shortly produce a range of vehicles that drastically reduced casualties.

Work began on building protected villages, based on the Malayan practice, to attempt to deny the insurgents food and succour. This was not a particular success because, instead of raising a local African militia, for fear of its subversion, the task of protecting the villages fell on the under-strength district administrators of Internal Affairs.

The Rhodesian security forces had lost one of the keys to their earlier successes: the willingness of the rural Africans to report the presence of insurgents. In this change of attitude, violent intimidation certainly played a part. The question remains: if theirs was a popular cause, why was it necessary for ZANU and ZAPU from the outset to impose their will on the Rhodesian African population by murder, massacre and mutilation? This has undermined the political superstructure from the early 1960s to this day. That said, having lacked willing recruits and having relied on press-ganging, both movements benefited because the rejection of the Home–Smith agreement prompted a steady flow of young recruits. This, however, was not a universal African reaction as the Rhodesian security forces were swamped by eager recruits whenever they raised new units, such as the Second Battalion the Rhodesian African Rifles and the Guard Force or expanded existing units like the police Support Unit.

In an attempt to compensate for this loss of information, in 1973 the Rhodesian security forces copied the British ploy in the war in Kenya against the Mau Mau of using pseudo-gangs to uncover the whereabouts of the insurgents. Counselled by Kenyan veterans, the Rhodesian security forces recruited trackers, linguists and other experts to form the Selous Scouts, whose primary purpose was pseudo-warfare, 'turning' captured insurgents to help them find their quarry.

The Rhodesian Air Force developed pilots skilled in aerial reconnaissance, in identifying signs of insurgent presence, camps and tracks. The ground forces cross-grained the country, looking for spoor. Intercepted radio messages told of insurgent intentions, as did captured insurgents or couriers.

Once certain of the presence of an insurgent group, a method was required of quickly snaring and eliminating it. The Alouette III offered a means of quickly inserting four-man stop groups on likely escape routes to isolate and eliminate the insurgents. The helicopter had been used in the earlier operations to leapfrog trackers along a spoor to shorten the pursuit. Tactics like dummy drops (feigning the dropping of troops) kept the pursued confused. Armed light aircraft, such as the AL60-B2L Trojan and Percival Provost T52, had been used to both attack or to mask the sound of the pursuing helicopters. Command from the air had been practised during operations in Mozambique.

What changed in early 1974 was the acquisition of the French Matra MG151 20mm cannon and its custom-built mounting which allowed the Rhodesians to convert some of their Alouette IIIs into command gunships, named K-Cars as opposed to the troop-carrying and general purpose 'G-Cars'. The clandestine acquisition of more Alouettes and the reinforcement by South African ones allowed the Rhodesian security forces to form three 'Fireforces', based at forward airfields at places like Mount Darwin and Mtoko (now Mutoko).

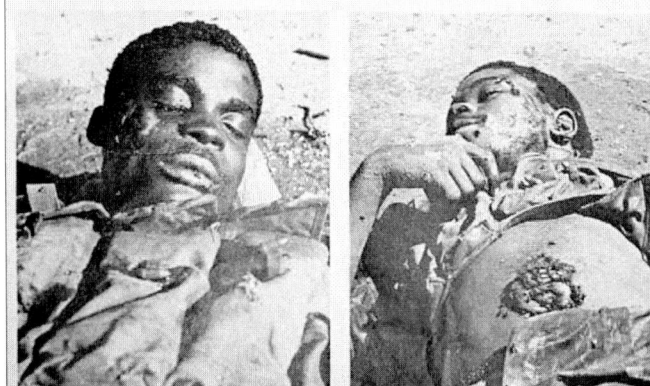

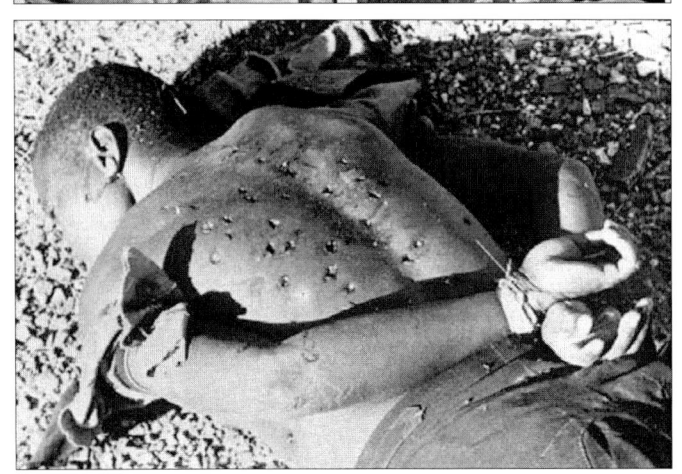

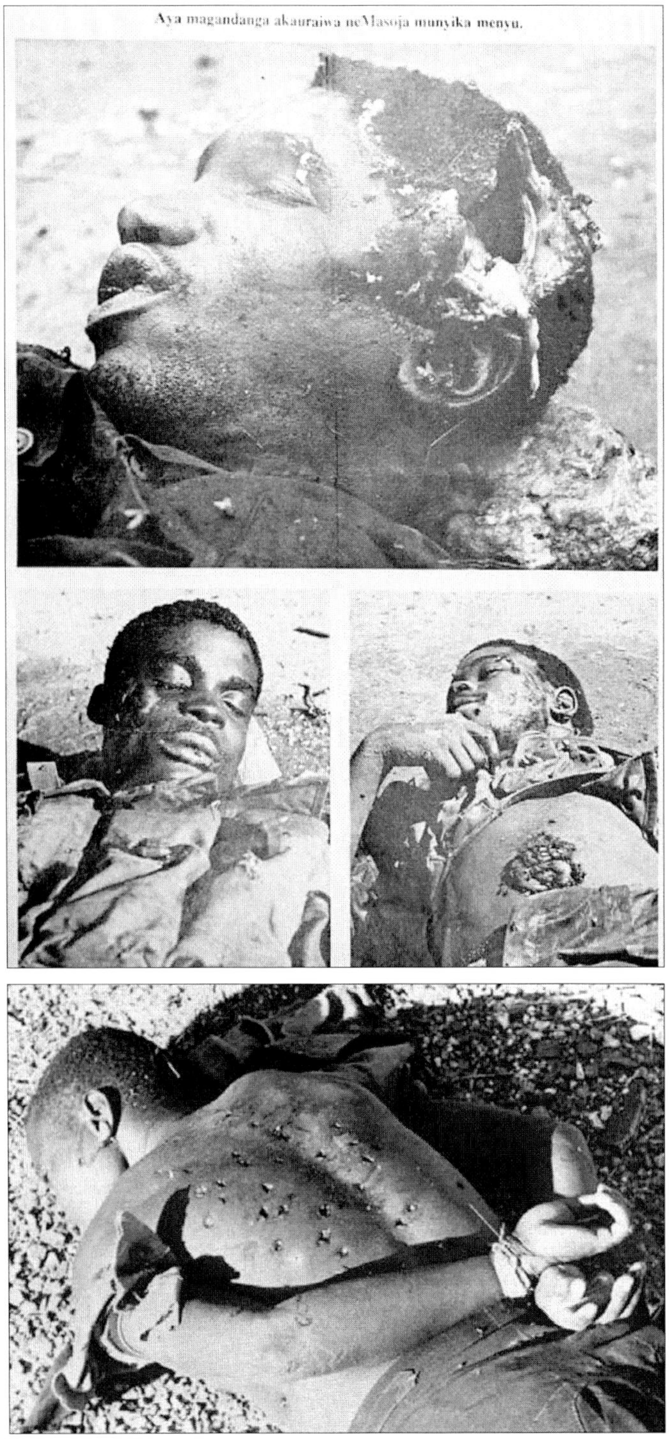

Murder and mutilation, courtesy of ZANLA.
Photo: Rhodesian Ministry of Information

Alouette G-Car insertions of four-man stop groups.
Photo: The Saints

CHAPTER THREE: THE AFRICAN NATIONALIST REVOLT, THE *CHIMURENGA*, AND THE RHODESIAN RESPONSE

AL60 B2L Trojan.
Photo: Winds of Destruction

Percival Provost T52 with armaments.
Photo: Winds of Destruction

French Matra MG151 20mm cannon.
Photo: Max T

A Fireforce normally consisted of a K-Car, bearing the commander of the ground forces and flown by the senior pilot, and three G-Cars carrying a total of twelve experienced regular troops drawn from the RLI or RAR. In support would fly a Trojan or a Provost in a reconnaissance or attack role, both being armed with 37mm SNEB rockets and the Provost also with twin Browning Mk II .303in machine guns and a range of light bombs. As techniques evolved with experience gained in controlling men from the air and with the 20mm cannon accounting for 60 per cent of casualties, Fireforce soon became a potent force. Indeed, it greatly aided the elimination of ZANLA insurgents within Rhodesia who by the end of 1974 were reduced to some 60 men confined to the eastern African communal areas (or tribal trust lands as they were entitled). Once there was a positive sighting, often by Selous Scouts manning observation posts (OPs) hidden in the hills, the Fireforce commander and the K-Car pilot would

Rhodesian forward airfields.
Photo: The Saints

Top: Dalmation four-gun 'fit'. *Photo: Max T.*; above: twin Browning Mk II .303in machine gun. *Photo: Tom Argyle*

RLI observation post in Zambia.
Photo: Dennis Croukamp

Middle: RLI convoy. *Photo C. MacIntosh*; above: RLI and Selous Scout column in Mozambique. *Photo: Dennis Croukamp*

plan their route to the target and the action thereafter, such as where to position stop groups. One consideration was to conceal the sound of the approaching helicopters by them being flown low to use the terrain to mask it. Another was where to send the 'land tail' convoy. Since it would carry second-wave troops, helicopter fuel and spare ammunition. The land tail had to be close enough to the action to allow rapid reinforcement of the three initial stop groups.

After briefing the aircrews and stick leaders, the commander and senior pilot would board the K-Car and lead the Fireforce into the air. En route the commander would take last-minute instructions from the OP on the precise position of the quarry. As the rural people were accustomed to the sight and sound of light aircraft flying on reconnaissance and other flights, the Fireforce pilot might order the Trojan, a particularly noisy aircraft, to fly ahead to conceal the sound of the helicopter engines.

Ten minutes or so out from the target, the K-Car would accelerate ahead and, guided by the OP, visually identify the target. It would climb to 800 feet above ground (the 20mm cannon was calibrated to fire at that height) and, orbiting to the left to bring the cannon to bear, open fire to kill or to drive the insurgents to ground. While the K-Car contained the insurgents, the G-Cars would deposit the stop groups in their prescribed positions and then depart to collect the second wave. Directed by the K-Car, the second wave would form a sweepline to mop up the survivors. A problem nevertheless was that too often the insurgents escaped before the stop groups were in place or before there were sufficient men on the ground to block all escape routes. This was addressed in the subsequent phase of the counter-insurgency campaign.

The next phase, 1974–1977, which featured Operation *Dingo*, began with the loss of Portugal as an ally after the 'Carnation Revolution', the military coup in Lisbon on 25 April 1974. This opened the entire eastern and southeastern border with Mozambique to ZANLA. As ZAPU's ZPRA was already infiltrating Rhodesia's western Matabeleland Province from Botswana, Rhodesia was left with only one secure border, that with South Africa.

Furthermore, Vorster had grown tired of supporting Rhodesia and, hoping he could reach an accommodation with the rest of Africa, forced Smith's hand by announcing the withdrawal of the South African Police and by interrupting the ammunition supply to Rhodesia. In December 1974, Smith was compelled to agree to a ceasefire with ZAPU and ZANU and to proposed negotiations in Lusaka. This happened when ZANLA in particular faced defeat and ZPRA was hardly involved. The ceasefire was a farce and the negotiations were stillborn. Vorster pressed Smith into further fruitless negotiations while the Portuguese abandoned Mozambique with long-time residents fleeing after Samora Machel, the FRELIMO president, nationalized land in accord with the Marxist dictum of 'seizing the means of production'. He would shortly close the ports of Beira and Maputo to Rhodesian traffic and declare war against Rhodesia. The flight of the Portuguese gained Rhodesia some immigrants, some of whom clandestinely flew in Alouette III helicopters and Britten-Norman Islander light twin-engined aircraft which were impressed into Rhodesian service. More Portuguese immigrants fled the Angolan civil war and the Soviet/Cuban intervention in 1975. The latter provoked an American response, part of which was the CIA-inspired Operation *Savannah*, a South African incursion from South West Africa (later Namibia) in November 1975. South Africa had been provoked by border incidents and the prospect of the South West Africa People's Organization (SWAPO) that she had been fighting since 1966, securing a safe haven in a Soviet client state. Although the disowning of the South African action by the Americans amid an international uproar led to a rapid and somewhat humiliating withdrawal, Vorster believed he had a friend in Kissinger. Together they chose to tackle Smith.

Having gained secure bases in Mozambique in 1975, ZANU had ZANLA concentrate on politicizing the rural Africans. By contrast, ZAPU and ZPRA continued to prefer to wait, with the intention of wresting the ultimate prize from ZANU after the latter's victory. As ZANLA recovered its strength, fed by idealistic young African recruits crossing Rhodesia's porous border, the insurgency revived. This bleak prospect for the whites induced many to emigrate, yet the most exposed whites, the farmers, remained on their land and 6,000 would still be there after 1980.

At considerable cost and in spite of the financial restraints, the Rhodesian Corps of Engineers expanded a *cordon sanitaire* of fencing and landmines from the Zambezi River right down the eastern and southeastern border eventually to the Limpopo River.

Despite the international arms embargo which ruled out any prospect of replacing its ageing jet aircraft, the Rhodesian Air Force, managed to clandestinely purchase and import a new light aircraft, the twin-engined Reims-Cessna 337, or 'Lynx', a civilian development of an earlier model used in forward air control in the Vietnam War. Once modified for military use, the Lynx replaced the Trojan, enhancing the Fireforce.

The embargo, of course, also affected the acquisition of armaments and munitions, making it necessary to obtain from the black market the 20mm and 30mm cannon shells, the 68mm Matra rockets for the Vampires and Hunters and the 37mm SNEB rockets for the Trojan, Provost and Lynx.

Bombs were manufactured locally. The first of the range was the Mk I wire-bound 20lb bomb fitted with a proximity fuse. The Provost could hang a pair under its wings but the Canberra was designed to carry the conventional load of 250-, 500- and 1,000lb bombs for destroying hard targets like bridges, fortifications and the like. To give it an anti-personnel counter-insurgency role, the air force's technical staff designed a cradle to fit in the bomb bay to carry 96 of the 20lb bombs with which to saturate a target. The delivery of the bombs, however, presented three problems. Firstly, accuracy demanded bombing from a low height above ground but not lower than 1,500 feet because the exploding bombs could damage the aircraft. 1,500 feet, however, was the perfect height for the Soviet SAM-7 Strela missile that FRELIMO, ZANLA and ZPRA were acquiring. 1,500 feet was also well within range of their anti-aircraft guns. The second problem was that the bomb pattern tended to be linear rather than smothering the target. Thirdly, the unseen danger was that the bombs could collide in the immediate turbulence created by the opening of the bomb doors and explode prematurely. This happened on 4 April 1974, destroying Canberra No. 2155 and killing Air Sub-Lieutenants Keith Goddard and Richard Airey. The suspension of the use of the bomb robbed the Canberra of a counter-insurgency role. It was reduced to carrying the 250lb, 500lb and 1,000lb range, useful for destroying bunkers, bridges and other hard targets.

With the war intensifying in 1976 the air force needed the Canberra back in action. The air force design team, led by Group Captain Peter Petter-Bowyer, director of projects, and Squadron

Reims-Cessna 337 or 'Lynx'.
Photos: The Saints

British Electric Canberra bomber.
Photo: Winds of Destruction

Group Captain Peter Petter-Bowyer; below: the bomb he designed.
Sources: Peter Petter-Bowyer

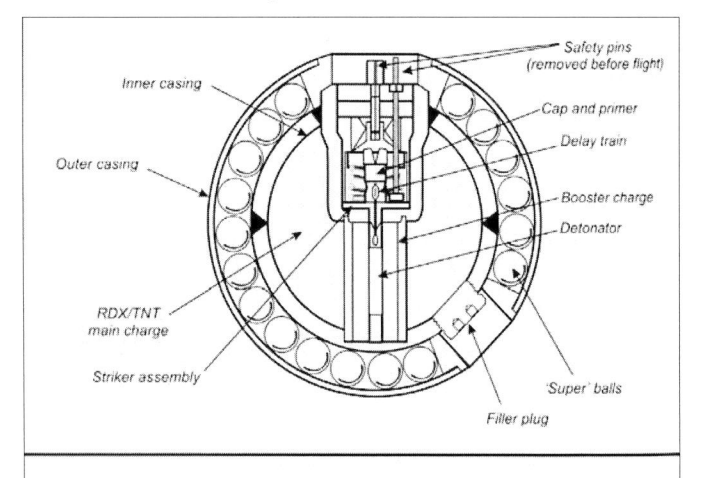

ALPHA – THE BOUNCING BOMB

Leader Ron Dyer, the Senior Officer Air Armaments, the air force's small armament section and a local engineering firm, Cochrane & Son, quickly produced the Mk II 'Alpha' bomb ('alpha' being the first of the new projects). It was based on Petter-Bowyer's idea of a 155mm double-hulled spherical steel bouncing bomb. The outer hull housed 250 super-rubber balls and the 87mm inner hull contained a three-pronged detonating pistol and RDX-TNT explosive. Given the poor aero-dynamic characteristics of round balls tumbling in the slipstreams of their neighbours, Petter-Bowyer calculated, and tests proved, that a mass release of 300 bombs would achieve the desired spread if the aircraft flew at 350 knots and 300 feet above ground. The super-rubber balls ensured that the bombs bounced forward on contact with the ground for 0.7 seconds before the detonator initiated the explosion at a height of two–three metres. Forty-five per cent of the casing would strike the target area (as opposed to 7.5 per cent of the conventional anti-personnel bomb). A key feature was that, although an explosion would result no matter which part of the bomb struck the ground, the detonator required a hard impact to be activated which made the bomb safe against accidental dropping during loading or when colliding with other bombs. The Canberra was fitted with six hoppers each holding 50 bombs. This allowed the crew to drop 50 bombs or a series of hoppers (with 0.6 seconds between each release) or all at once. A full release would cover an area of 100 metres wide and 700 metres long. These bombs devastated the targeted camps on *Dingo* and on other operations and restored a counter-insurgency role for the Canberra. Both ZANLA and ZPRA greatly feared the Alpha bomb.

The seventh in the series of projects, the Golf bomb, was equally fearsome. It was a cylindrical 450kg (1,000lb) percussion and shrapnel bomb. It was double-skinned with the space between the steel skins filled with 71,000 pieces of chopped steel bar. The inner skin was filled with ANFO (ammonium nitrate pellets mixed with diesel) high-velocity explosive. For maximum effect, the ANFO was ignited by a detonator at the end of a 984mm long probe containing pentolite (a 50/50 mixture of Pentaerythritol tetranitrate, or PENT, and TNT, achieving a detonation velocity of 7,400 metres a second) and connected by a cordtex detonating cord (burning at 2,000 metres a second) to a second pentolite detonator in the tail.

The effect of the simultaneous double pentolite detonations was to compress the ANFO explosion, achieving maximum sideways effect. The 2,745 metre-per-second shockwave would stun at 120 metres. It produced a spherical bush-clearing pattern to 90 metres and 135 metres long. The Golf bomb's safety distance was a kilometre if troops were behind solid cover and two kilometres if they were in the open. The safety height was 2,000 feet above

Lynx pilot covering fire during a low-level bombing run or 37mm rocket attack.

Accuracy in target marking was also a problem. This was solved by screwing into the body of the 37mm SNEB rocket a mild steel tubular extension, filled with 200 grams of white phosphorus, between the propellant section and the explosive warhead. In practice it was found that this innovation not only marked the target but also improved the fragmentation of the warhead. This inspired Petter-Bowyer's team to fill one of these extensions with 100 grams of TNT, producing the 'Long Tom' rocket with a tenfold explosive effect. The Long Tom was slower in flight but lost no accuracy or stability.

Used on Operation *Dingo* but rarely otherwise, the cheapest of Rhodesian weapons was invented by Peter Petter-Bowyer to increase the potency of the Hunter. Costing less than 50 cents to produce, it was simply a headless six-inch nail equipped with three plastic fins. 4,500 darts were packed head to tail in a four-panelled, streamlined fibreglass dispenser. Armed with two dispensers, a Hunter pilot would begin a dive at 450 knots, line up the target with his gun sight and release the dispensers. Half a second later, explosive charges in the nose cones of the dispensers would blow open the panels, releasing the darts. Pushed apart by the slipstream of their neighbours, the darts would riddle an area 70 metres wide by 900 metres long. When used, except on *Dingo*, no one escaped a strike. The use of this silent killer was limited by the mistake of naming it a 'flechette' before it was realized that the 'flechette' rifle round was an internationally banned weapon. Consequently, it was used only where it would not attract publicity such as the remote Tembué camp on *Dingo*.

To enhance its capability, the Rhodesian Army formed new units: 2RAR, the Rhodesian Armoured Car Regiment, the Grey's Scouts (a mounted infantry unit), the Rhodesian Intelligence Corps and the Rhodesian Defence Regiment. The Guard Force was created to take over protection tasks.

To secure manpower for these and additional independent companies, the Rhodesian Government increased national service to two years. The BSAP strengthened its ranks with some of the national servicemen, as did the Rhodesian Air Force.

GOLF BOMB

ground. One of a pair of Golfs would be fitted with a vane, or later a parachute, to separate their detonations. A Hunter would release its Golfs at 4,500 feet during a 60-degree-angle, 400-knot dive and then endure a six-G pull out to avoid any shrapnel and fire from the ground.

The success of the Golf led to the production in 1978 of the scaled-down double-skinned 'Juliet' or mini-Golf bomb to enhance the striking power of the Lynx and therefore of the Fireforce. To allow the Lynx to reach safety, the mini-Golf deployed a parachute to arrest its fall and to achieve a vertical impact and the maximum sideways effect.

Because accuracy is important in counter-insurgency operations to avoid harming the uninvolved, the project team had turned their attention to napalm bombs that are notoriously wayward, being often little more than a drum. They replaced the unsatisfactory steel 17-gallon napalm bomb and its unpredictable bursting charge with a low-drag, glass-fibre-and-asbestos-moulded 16-gallon container with fins. Its igniters were two Alpha-bomb pistols to ensure detonation. This 'frantan' (frangible tank) bomb could be carried by the Lynx and dropped accurately with its flaming contents splashing forward.

As its lack of machine guns to suppress fire from the ground had confined the Trojan to rocket attacks, the project team equipped the new Lynx with a unique pair of over-wing gun pods, armed with .303in Browning Mk II machine guns. This allowed the

'Flechette', yet another of Petter-Bowyer's lethal inventions.
Photo: Peter Petter-Bowyer

Practice by 1976 had refined Fireforce tactics and hardened its troops, achieving an 80:1 kill rate. After an experiment in late 1976, using the SAS paratroops to increase the ability of Fireforce to deploy more men on the ground, all regular troops underwent parachute training. Consequently the Fireforces were reinforced with a C-47 'Dakota', each which could provide an instant reinforcement of 16–20 men. Rhodesian regulars became the most practised paratroopers in the world, jumping into action almost daily when on operations and on some occasions three times in a day. No other paratroopers have done that. In doing so they undermined the romantic myth of parachuting because it simply became a method of delivery.

The army continued to innovate in 1977. It had the Rhodesia Regiment form motorcycle platoons for quick reaction to attacks on farms and the like, for rapid reinforcement and cross-country movement, and for tasks such as patrolling the mined border (which continued to expand southward along the Mozambican border). The RR battalions also trained reconnaissance platoons for clandestine operations in Mozambique to gather information and to harass ZANLA and FRELIMO.

All this was giving Rhodesia hardened, experienced and self-reliant servicemen and made operations as daring as *Dingo* possible.

The growing presence of ZANU/ZANLA in the unsettled state of Mozambique where FRELIMO was trying to establish control in the wake of the Portuguese exodus presented a tempting target. Because Rhodesia was more exposed than ever to international pressure after the loss of her Portuguese ally, the Rhodesian Government feared a world reaction to the destruction of the strategic infrastructure of newly independent countries. It allowed, however, 'hot pursuit' operations since they were defined as legal by the Kellogg-Briand, or Paris Pact, of 1928 despite it renouncing war.

The first major raid was in October 1974 when the SAS destroyed a ZPRA camp and munitions dump in southern Zambia. In early 1976, after Samora Machel had declared war on Rhodesia and closed the rail links to the Mozambican ports, the Rhodesians attacked ZANLA staging posts for new infiltration routes in Mozambique's southeastern Gaza Province. The Selous Scouts and the air force attacked a position at Pafuri on the Limpopo River while the SAS did likewise at Mavue just beyond the Sabi–Lundi confluence.

In August 1976 a Selous Scout column of vehicles struck the main ZANLA base at Nyadzonya in the Manica Province of Mozambique, killing 1,200. This attack provoked the feared world outcry on the grounds that the base was claimed to be a refugee camp. It gave Vorster the excuse he and Kissinger needed to corner Smith. Vorster withdrew his helicopter pilots from Rhodesia, the only South African servicemen still deployed there. Suddenly, railway congestion was contrived, holding up vital fuel and ammunition supplies. Rhodesian stocks were down to two weeks' supply when Smith conceded majority rule in a meeting with Kissinger on 23 September 1976.

The consequent Geneva Conference only produced a stalemate; fter rejecting a further set of proposals advanced by David Owen, the British Foreign Secretary and Cyrus Vance, the US Secretary of State, Ian Smith turned his back on the Anglo-Americans, as did Vorster, and pursued an internal settlement with Bishop Muzorewa, the Reverend Sithole and Senator Chief Chirau.

C-47 'Dakota'.
Photo: Tom Argyle

CHAPTER FOUR:
THE PLAN

Hoping to weaken Mugabe's position at the Geneva Conference, Ian Smith sanctioned Operation *Mardon* (30 October–5 November 1976), an attack by the SAS, Selous Scouts, RLI and RAR on nearby ZANLA targets in Mozambique's Tete, Manica/Sofala and Gaza Provinces. *Mardon* was followed by a short-range harassing campaign in Mozambique. There were, however, more tempting targets.

After Operation *Eland*, the attack by the Selous Scouts on Nyadzonya ZANLA base in August 1976, the Rhodesian security forces had kept ZANLA under surveillance through aerial photo-reconnaissance and intelligence gleaned from captured cadres and deserters. It soon became clear that ZANLA was building two large camp complexes, deeper in Mozambique, believing them to be beyond the reach of the Rhodesians. The main camp complex was at 'New Farm', 17 kilometres north of Chimoio (once Vila Pery). Straddling the main road and the railway to the port of Beira, Chimoio is a small town 90 kilometres directly east of the Rhodesian border city of Umtali. 'New Farm' had been, until 1975, 'Monte de Graça Farm', founded and developed in the 1960s by Lieutenant-Colonel Jacob Johannes 'Oom Japie' Pienaar, a former South African Army veteran. He grew cotton, maize, tobacco and sunflowers until he and his family were forced off the farm by FRELIMO and ZANLA, leaving behind all his farming vehicles, equipment and implements.

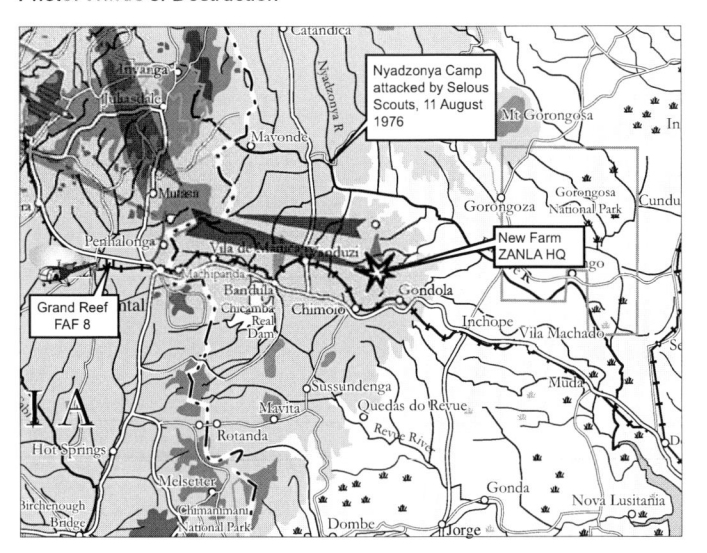

With an overall population of 4,000 recruits, trained cadres, convalescents and camp followers, New Farm was the main ZANLA holding and training centre, receiving both recruits brought out of Rhodesia and personnel returning from advanced training in Tanzania, China and Ethiopia. It was also the most tempting target because it housed ZANLA's operational, administrative and logistical headquarters with offices for Mugabe, Josiah Tongogara, the commander of ZANLA, and his deputy, Rex Nhongo (the *nom de guerre* of the now-retired Lieutenant-General Solomon Mujuru) and their staff. This headquarters controlled ZANLA's activities in Mozambique's central Manica Province, distributing reinforcements and supplies for operations in eastern and southeastern Rhodesia.

The second base seemed secure from attack as it was tucked away at Tembué, a village near the Mozambican–Malawian border, northwest of Tete town and some 200 kilometres away

The first photograph of Nyadzonya with over 800 ZANLA cadres mustered on the parade ground and a further 200 visible among the buildings. The river on the right is the Nyadzonya.
Photo: Winds of Destruction

Top left: Josiah Tongogara; top right: Rex Nhongo; above left: Major Brian Robinson; above right: Group Captain Norman Walsh.

from the Rhodesian northeastern border. It held trained cadres and trainees.

The limited success of *Mardon* and an air photograph of 700 men on the rifle range at Chimoio, coupled with news of the growth of Tembué, prompted Major Brian Robinson, the SAS commander, and Group Captain Norman Walsh BCR (Bronze Cross of Rhodesia), a decorated pilot and the current Director of Air Operations, to devise a daring joint air force and airborne SAS attack on New Farm and, to preserve the surprise, followed a day or so later, by an assault on Tembué. They chose a joint air and ground attack because Rhodesia's remaining hard-worked jet aircraft had been reduced by age and accidents to nine Hunters, six Vampires and four or five Canberra bombers—insufficient to deliver a crushing blow to the sprawling ZANLA complexes. The addition of troops to mop up meant they could also gather vital information, take prisoners and destroy war matériel.

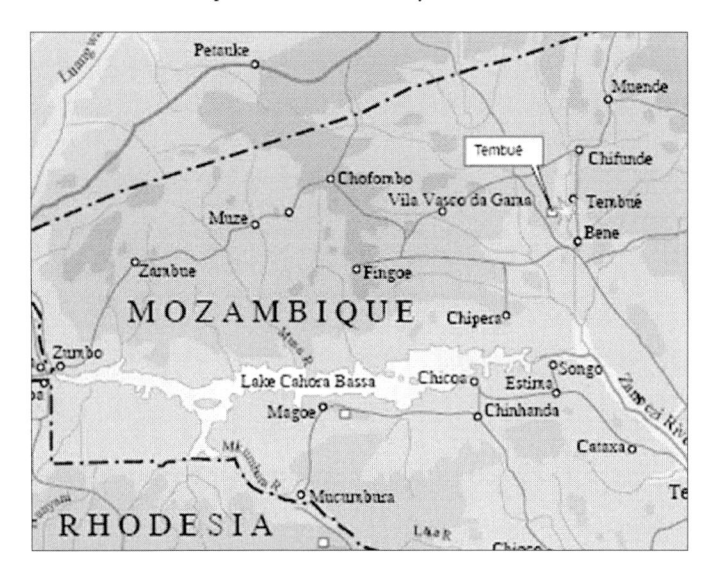

The plan was hard to sell for various reasons. The 'hot pursuit' policy meant that air support for external operations had been ruled out by the Rhodesian Government to avoid provoking world reaction. This meant that only casualty evacuation by air had been allowed on Operations *Eland* and *Mardon*.

In any case, New Farm, let alone Tembué, was outside the range of the Alouette III. It could get there but not return. An Alouette G-Car with a crew of two, four fully equipped troops and 400lbs of fuel in its tank could fly for 45 minutes. The K-Car with its crew of two or three, its 20mm cannon and ammunition, and 600lbs of fuel had an endurance of 75–100 minutes. It meant that fuel would have to be dropped by parachute into a secure location (called an 'administration area') in Mozambique along with 16 men armed with two 81mm mortars to protect it.

Another limitation was the number of troops available in November 1976. The RLI had yet to be trained as paratroopers, which meant that Robinson would have to rely on his 100 or so SAS operators and some 40 1RLI helicopter-borne troops to cover the widely dispersed camps within the complexes without the support of heavy weapons or any reserves. ZANLA had learned from the Selous Scouts' raid on Nyadzonya to disperse its personnel. The rolling, heavily wooded terrain of New Farm held 17 camps scattered over 25 square kilometres. The headquarters were housed in the farmhouse, buildings and sheds of J.J. Pienaar. The growing camps comprised hundreds of traditional African circular thatched pole and *dagga* (mud-daubed) huts, larger square thatched structures and numerous tents and shelters. In addition, the camps were surrounded by intricate patterns of trenches, dug-in anti-aircraft weapons and an early warning system of towers for sentries with whistles.

The Tembué complex housed the ZANLA Command Headquarters for Tete Province and their general training and specialist skills training centre. It comprised three hutted camps (A, B and C), along the east bank of the Luia River, a tributary of the Capoche River which flows southward into the Zambezi River east of the Cabora Bassa Dam. By July 1977, because the camps offered training in heavy weapons, it was known that two DShK 12.7mm machine guns, two KPV Soviet 14.5mm anti-aircraft guns, one 82mm mortar and a 75mm recoilless rifle defended Camp A. Camp B had one heavy machine gun, two 14.5mm anti-aircraft guns and two 75mm recoilless rifles.

This was clearly not a task for the faint-hearted, considering that the SAS would have to parachute into New Farm reinforced by the 40 RLI troopers, to assault its 5,000 inmates, withdraw, rearm and a day later attack the 2,000 inhabitants of Tembué before they heard of the fate of New Farm.

Not surprisingly, when Robinson and Walsh put the proposal to the Special Operations Committee in November 1976, it was turned down. Group Captain Peter Petter-Bowyer recalls that the proposal "frightened those who listened because they were madly daring and, potentially, incredibly dangerous".[1] The arguments against it were various. The critics felt the 16-man force was inadequate protection of the jet fuel cached to allow the helicopters to shuttle home the troops. Any loss of the fuel or of helicopters could leave troops stranded deep in Mozambique. Furthermore a significant loss of irreplaceable jet aircraft could render the Rhodesian Air Force impotent. There were worries expressed about an international uproar evoking further pressure on Rhodesia once the camps had inevitably been depicted by ZANU and FRELIMO as housing refugees.

The plan to attack Chimoio and then far-off Tembué was dismissed as impractical.

Undeterred, Robinson and Walsh persisted. They repeatedly resubmitted the plan during the following twelve months as aerial reconnaissance showed the growth of the camps at New Farm and Tembué to accommodate the increasing numbers of recruits and trained personnel returning from Tanzania and elsewhere. In June 1977 they suggested the next moon phase should be exploited. In July 1977 they proposed to strengthen the attacking force with newly trained RLI paratroopers. The attack was provisionally scheduled for late August to take advantage of the moon phase, full moon being on 28 August.

---

[1] P.J.H. Petter-Bowyer, *Winds of Destruction: The Autobiography of a Rhodesian Combat Pilot*, 30° South Publishers, Johannesburg, 2005, p. 306

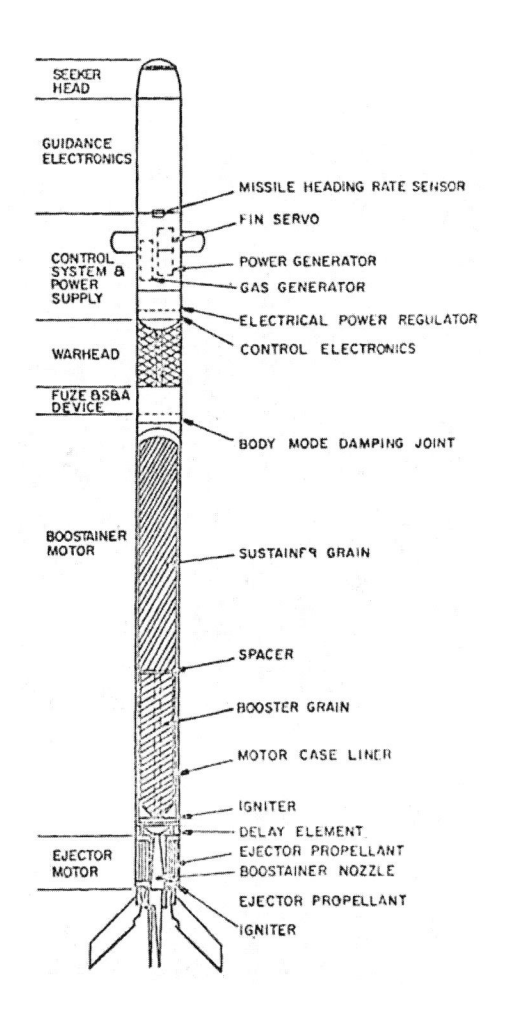

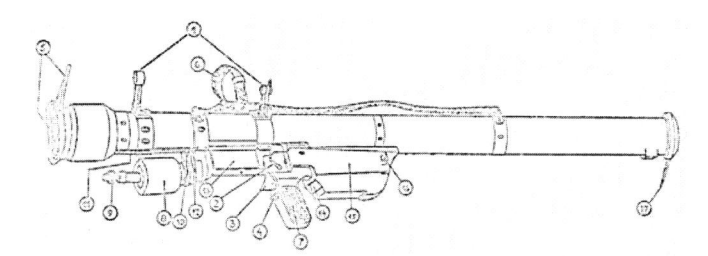

Above and bottom left: Soviet Strela SAM-7 light infrared seeking missile. *Photo: Winds of Destruction*

A Frelimo Soviet-manufactured T-34 tank.
Photo: Jon Caffin

Their version of the plan, submitted on 11 August 1977, envisaged withdrawing troops by Dakotas from Tembué after mortar teams from Support Commando, 1RLI, had secured two local airstrips, the first at Tembué village and the second airstrip at a nearby Zambian road-builders' camp. The first would be taken from its FPLM garrison by a helicopter-borne team. A twin-engined Britten Norman Islander light aircraft would land the second team on the road-builders' strip. Their secondary purpose was to deny ZANLA and the FPLM the use of road-builders' vehicles. This idea would not feature in the final plan.

The plan resubmitted in mid-November 1977 had been updated by Captain Scott McCormack, the SAS intelligence officer, and the SAS and air force command elements from air photographs supplied by the Joint Services Photographic Intelligence Service (JSPIS) and intelligence from captured ZANLA personnel.

It took into account the decision by Mozambique's president, Samora Machel, to post members of his armed forces, *Forças Populares para o Libertação de Moçambique* (FPLM), into the ZANLA's camps to give him a measure of control over them as well as increasing their protection. At the same time, he allowed ZANLA to share his logistical services and transport and, for further mutual protection, stationed FPLM units nearby. Some of these were mobile and armed with anti-aircraft weapons including the Russian Strela SAM-7 light infrared seeking missile. The mobile units would fan out along the roads near the camps to attempt to bring down attacking aircraft. There was, however, no threat from the fledgling Mozambican air force based at Beira and Nacala, both ports on the Indian Ocean. The FPLM protection of 'New Farm' Chimoio was logically more intensive than that of the remote camp at Tembué because it bordered the relatively developed road–rail corridor from Beira to Umtali. New Farm had a 100-man FPLM garrison. To its immediate south, 17 kilometres away, in Chimoio town was the FPLM brigade headquarters with 100 Soviet advisers, 400 FPLM and 100 Tanzanian troops, armed and equipped with mortars, trucks, anti-tank and anti-aircraft weapons, including SAM-7s, armoured personnel carriers and T-34/-54 tanks. Half an hour away westward by road from New Farm was an FPLM platoon at Vanduzi, armed with mortars and anti-aircraft weapons. Closer to the Rhodesian border was an FPLM battalion headquarters at Vila de Manica with 725 FLPM and 110 Tanzanian troops, vehicles, anti-tank and anti-aircraft guns, and the SAM-7. Almost at the Rhodesian border, at Machipanda, was an FPLM company armed with the SAM-7 and other anti-aircraft weapons. Vila de Manica was an hour and a half's drive to ZANLA's New Farm and Machipanda two hours', so their garrisons could not quickly reinforce it but they posed a danger to overflying aircraft, particularly during the vulnerable troop withdrawal by slow-flying helicopters. The overall FPLM presence and paucity of roads ruled out any chance of a ground withdrawal by vehicle, which made the Rhodesian attack all the more dangerous. In August 1976, after the Selous Scouts' attack on Nyadzonya (Operation *Eland*), a couple of troopers had been left behind and had walked to safety in Rhodesia through an unguarded border. The distance of Chimoio from Rhodesia made a similar feat improbable and had to be taken into account by Robinson and Walsh and their team.

The remoteness of Tembué made aerial recovery essential. The three ZANLA camps there, however, did not have such strong support on hand apart from the 150-man FPLM company, armed with mortars and anti-aircraft guns at Tembué village two kilometres north of the complex. Twenty minutes away by road to the south was Bene, guarded by ten men with rifles. The battalion headquarters was at Fingoe, three hours away to the west, with 450 men, anti-tank guns, mortars and vehicles. Another 150-man company, armed with anti-aircraft guns and mortars, was based at Furançungo, three hours to the east of Tembué. The brigade headquarters was six hours away on the main road to the southeast at Tete, the provincial capital. Stationed there were 600 troops, anti-aircraft guns and SAM-7s, mortars and vehicles.

By 10 November 1977, when the SAS–air force plan was revised yet again, both ZANLA camp complexes posed even more formidable targets as they had grown to accommodate the influx of trainees and trained personnel. New Farm was believed to have a population of 9,000–10,000 and Tembué 4,000, all protected by significant anti-aircraft weaponry. Nevertheless, Robinson and Walsh were confident of success, and argued that it was necessary to attack them before the task was made more difficult by the coming heavy rainy season and to prevent ZANLA's intention to mount a massive infiltration into Rhodesia. Their aims therefore were to disrupt the reinforcement and resupply of ZANLA groups within Rhodesia by inflicting the maximum casualties and destroying war matériel except for specific items such as SAM-7 missiles and launchers, and to gather intelligence on ZANLA's intentions.

Co-incidentally Lieutenant-Colonel Ron Reid-Daly of the Selous Scouts had arrived at the same conclusion regarding ZANLA's intentions and presented a plan for Operation *Virile*, a vehicle-borne, bridge-blowing exercise in the Mozambican hinterland to hamper that infiltration.

Robinson and Walsh were aided by the Rhodesian meteorological service having succeeded in hacking into the Intelsat satellite weather transmissions to Europe and obtaining a cloud map each morning by 1000hrs. The hacking was necessary because Rhodesia's international pariah status had excluded her from obtaining the information legally. It meant, however, that Rhodesia had access to better weather data than those traditionally supplied by her ground stations and those in neighbouring African territories.

To attack both targets, the jet aircraft would initially fly out of their home bases: the Hunters out of Thornhill, Gwelo and the Canberras and Vampires from New Sarum in Salisbury and then all of them would return to New Sarum to refuel and rearm.

For the rear base from which to mount 'Zulu 1', the attack on New Farm, Chimoio, the planning team chose Grand Reef airfield, 20 kilometres west of Umtali, as its landing strip was long enough for a Dakota. The six Dakotas carrying paratroops would depart from the air force's main base at New Sarum and after the parachute drop fly back to Grand Reef. They would be refuelled and made ready to fly out to New Farm with reserve paratroops, fuel, ammunition and equipment as needed or to Salisbury with casualties brought in by helicopter.

Hawker Hunters in flight.
Photo: Winds of Destruction

Hawker Hunter displaying full armaments.
Photo: Winds of Destruction

A seventh Dakota, fitted out with radios and secure teleprinters to act as a flying tactical command post for Lieutenant-General Peter Walls, would likewise refuel at Grand Reef as would the Lynx light aircraft, flying in reconnaissance and support roles.

The picnic grounds at Lake Alexander (40 kilometres north of Umtali, on the Odzani River in the mountains overlooking Mozambique) were chosen as the helicopter assembly area with fuel, supplies and a medical resuscitation station. From there would depart 31 helicopters, consisting of a command G-Car, ten K-Cars, ten G-Cars carrying 40 2 Commando 1RLI troopers, ten South African G-Cars (codenamed 'Polo') carrying an air force commander, air force technicians, the RLI doctor and a medic, Special Branch (SB) members (to handle any prisoners), two 81mm mortar crews of Support Commando 1RLI with their tubes and bombs, plus aircraft and other spares for quick repairs.

The Polo G-Cars would peel off to the left when the helicopter fleet neared New Farm and fly northward to establish the 'administration area' (admin area) for refuelling helicopters,

Vampire in flight.
Photo: Winds of Destruction

Vampire undergoing mechanical checks, displaying some of its armaments.
Photo: Winds of Destruction

Lake Alexander.
Photo: Richard Perry

receiving prisoners and immediate stabilization of the wounded. The site of the admin area would be in an unpopulated area some 20 kilometres north of New Farm. The arrival of the admin-area team would be followed by the delivery by parachute of drums of aviation fuel dropped from a Douglas DC-7 cargo aircraft supplied by Jack Malloch. The owner of Afretair, a sanctions-breaking airline, Malloch was a veteran pilot who had flown Spitfire Mk IXs over wartime Italy with Ian Smith as his flight commander. The admin area would provide a protected landing ground for the G-Cars while they waited for calls to evacuate battle casualties and for the withdrawal phase. The fuel would allow the Alouette K-Cars to provide continuous air support for the troops on the ground.

The other 21 helicopters would fly on toward New Farm, aiming to arrive just after the attack on New Farm by three Hunters, bombing and strafing the ZANLA headquarters and the nearby camps, and by four Vampires firing rockets at and strafing the recruits' camp some distance to the north. The airstrike would be timed to catch the ZANLA personnel on their early morning muster parades. Thirty seconds later four Canberras, each dropping 300 Mk II Alpha bombs, would begin a low level bombing run over most of the camps. A minute and a half later, taking advantage of the distraction caused by the airstrike, and covered by four Hunters diving in to suppress anti-aircraft fire, two sections of three Dakotas each would start their delivery of their 96 SAS and 48 3 Commando 1RLI, paratroops who would form two sides of a 'box' to attempt to block off escape routes to the southwest, south and southeast. As the paratroops touched down, ten G-Cars would land their 40 2 Commando men along the third side on the northwest. Lacking sufficient troops to close the fourth or northern side of the 25-square-kilometre complex, Robinson and Walsh proposed to use the 20mm cannons of the ten K-Cars to close the trap.

As the troops shed their parachutes, Walsh, flying the command G-Car, would take control of the restriking aircraft while Robinson co-ordinated the troops as they swept inward. The troops would mop up, destroy matériel and recover what they could before being withdrawn by a helicopter shuttle via the admin area to Lake Alexander and Grand Reef airfield. Those who were assigned to the attack on Tembué, the SAS and the Support Commando troopers, would be flown back to New Sarum, Salisbury, by the Dakotas to draw fresh parachutes, to be briefed and to prepare themselves for the next task. The helicopter fleet would fly northward to Mount Darwin, carrying the 3 Commando troops who were to form the parachute reserve and the 2 Commando men who would provide the protection troops for the first refuelling stops on the way to Tembué. The helicopters would spend the night at Mount Darwin before flying on to the Rhodesian Army camp of Chiswiti.

Because Mount Darwin, 130 kilometres north-northeast of Salisbury, had a runway long enough for Dakotas, it was chosen as the rear base for the Dakotas and Lynxes and the 48 3 Commando paratroops to form the reserve for 'Zulu 2'. Chiswiti was north of there and just south of the Mozambican border. It would serve as the helicopter assembly point with prepositioned fuel, ammunition and other supplies and a medical resuscitation unit. As the distance to Tembué was three times of that to Chimoio, an interim refuelling point, designated the 'Staging Post' would be 50 kilometres north of Chiswiti on the 'Guard's Van' of 'The Train', an elongated mountain range, resembling a steam locomotive and a line of carriages, running east of the small village of Magoe and parallel to the southern shore of the Cabora Bassa Dam on the Zambezi River. Having deposited a technical and medical team and protection troops with mortars, and once refuelled, the helicopter fleet would fly 130 kilometres northeastward to the target. The G-Cars would land at the admin area eleven kilometres in the hills west of the Tembué complex. They would be carrying the air force commander, technicians, SB members and medics. The K-Cars and the command G-Car, flown again by Walsh and carrying Robinson, would fly on to attack the target before returning to the admin area to refuel and rearm from the drums and ammunition parachuted in by the DC-7. On this occasion, the protection troops, armed with the lighter 60mm mortar, would also parachute in from the DC-7.

As at New Farm, Chimoio, by the time the K-Cars and the command helicopter arrived over the three-camp complex, the Hunters and Vampires would have rocketed and strafed it, followed by the Canberras disgorging their bouncing Alpha bombs. Unlike the attack on New Farm, there would be no helicopter-borne troops, just boxes around the two southern camps formed by the SAS and Support Commando paratroops. Supported by the K-Cars and with the Hunters, Vampires and Lynxes on call and orbiting high above out of range of any fire from the ground, the troops would sweep the camps, destroying them and any irrecoverable weapons and equipment. After mopping up, the helicopter shuttle would begin carrying troops back home via the 'Train'.

Everything, of course, depended on maximum secrecy, lest the camps be empty, and a large helping of luck if this daring, almost reckless plan, was to produce a success.

CHAPTER FIVE:
THE GO-AHEAD FOR OPERATION *DINGO*

In mid-November 1977 Major Brian Robinson and Group Captain Norman Walsh could be forgiven if they wearied of presenting their plan when, instead of it, the proposal for Operation *Virile* by the Selous Scouts was accepted by Combined Operations (ComOps). *Virile*'s D-Day was set for Sunday, 20 November 1977. Robinson and Walsh knew that both could not be mounted simultaneously because the Rhodesian Air Force lacked sufficient strike aircraft to support them. It had to be one or the other. A reversal of the decision would surprise them.

It was not as if Lieutenant-Colonel Ron Reid-Daly had not also been exasperated by the decision-making process. He had been discouraged in 1975 when he had been refused permission to destroy eleven Mozambican bridges.[2] One of the reasons was that President Machel had not yet closed Rhodesia's access to his ports. Machel would do so in March 1976 and the Rhodesian Government had allowed 'hot pursuit' operations. Since the beginning of 1977, complementing SAS ambush, mining and other operations elsewhere in Mozambique, Reid-Daly had been allowed to use his Selous Scouts successfully to harass ZANLA's lines of communications in the Gaza Province of Mozambique and to end the use of the railway to bring infiltrators up to Rhodesia's southeastern border. After the Scouts' campaign of destruction of the Maputo–Malvernia railway line from early to mid-1977 had forced the ZANLA infiltrators to march and porter their supplies long distances to the Rhodesian border, Reid-Daly proposed to send in a column of vehicles to demolish five bridges in Mozambique behind the Rhodesian mountainous eastern border. His purpose was to deny ZANLA a logistics route from Chimoio to Espungabera, a border village in the southeast. Reid-Daly argued that, after the bridges were down, the alternative infiltration routes could easily be ambushed and mined. In addition, he pointed out, the imminent onset of the annual rainy season would swell rivers, further hampering the infiltrators. Despite the attacks on the railway, the demolition of bridges was still, however, defined as an attack on the economic infrastructure of Mozambique outside the scope of 'hot pursuit'. The CIO and the Rhodesian Ministry of External Affairs, in particular, worried that it would spark further international outrage at a moment when Rhodesia was under pressure to accept the latest Anglo-American settlement proposals being foisted on her by David Owen and Cyrus Vance. Reid-Daly's Operation *Aztec*, a vehicle-borne

South African Prime Minister B. J. Vorster.

Senator Chief Jeremiah Chirau.

---

[2] Lt-Col Ron Reid-Daly, *Top Secret War*, Alberton, Galago, 1982, pp. 283–285.

attack on 31 May–4 June 1977 on the Gaza villages of Jorge do Limpopo, Mapai and Mabalane, had prompted international protests including one from B.J. Vorster. By late 1977, however, the Rhodesian Government did not expect the remote *Virile* bridges to attract any attention.

On Saturday, 19 November 1977, Ian Smith suddenly changed his mind and sanctioned Operation *Dingo*. In response, Lieutenant-General Walls postponed Operation *Virile* and ordered the halting of the Selous Scouts' column, en route to Espungabera under the command of Major (later a South African brigadier) Albert Sachse BCR. The column stopped at the resort of Hot Springs, near Birchenough Bridge, south of Umtali.

What had happened was that Smith had finally turned his back on the Anglo-American plan, which demanded the involvement of ZANU and ZAPU in any settlement, in favour of an accommodation with the internally based nationalist political parties on the basis of a transfer to majority rule within two years which he had promised Kissinger and Vorster on 23 September 1976.

These internal parties were led by two of his old foes, namely Bishop Muzorewa of the United African National Council Party and the Reverend Ndabaningi Sithole of his faction of ZANU, and by Chief Jeremiah Chirau of the Zimbabwe United People's Organization (ZUPO). With the backing of significant nationalists such as James Chikerema, a veteran insurgent leader and a ZAPU defector, whom Muzorewa had just made his new vice-chairman, Smith wanted to announce during a visit to Bulawayo on Friday, 25 November 1977, that the Rhodesian Government would hold a referendum in the new year to secure the sanction of the mainly white electorate of a new constitution based on universal adult suffrage. He would add that a general election based on that franchise would follow before the end of 1978. Smith hoped that, by conceding majority rule and therefore the return of an African-dominated government, Rhodesia would finally achieve international recognition and the lifting of the UN economic sanctions. If that happened, he believed that the new government could defeat the threatened Marxist takeover by Mugabe or Nkomo.

Before making that announcement, Smith chose to implement Operation *Dingo* in the hope that its double punch against the ZANLA concentrations at Chimoio and Tembué would stun and perhaps fatally weaken his main antagonist, Robert Mugabe.

Smith was also spurred on by the need to meet the increasing threat that ZANLA posed to Rhodesia's northeastern, eastern and southeastern areas. ZANLA groups were not only penetrating deep into Rhodesia, subverting the rural African populations, but were also harassing border posts and settlements. That very day, 19 November 1977, the southeastern border post was once again subjected to, albeit inaccurate, mortar and small-arms fire from neighbouring Malvernia. Rhodesian forces returned fire. This, perhaps, encouraged Nkomo's ZPRA to indulge in an unprovoked barrage of mortars, heavy machine guns and rifle fire across the Zambezi River against Rhodesian security forces' positions at Kanyemba on Monday, 21 November.

Although Smith clearly wanted his decision to settle kept a secret, James Chikerema on Monday, 21 November betrayed something of the direction being taken. Decrying the apparent British support for Nkomo, Chikerema announced to the press that he was going to London to tell Dr Owen that the British Government was treacherous, gutless and had no role to play in the settlement process because it lacked the power to enforce anything.

CHAPTER SIX:
THE BRIEFING FOR THE ATTACK ON NEW FARM, CHIMOIO

Ian Smith's order to go ahead with Operation *Dingo*, with its D-Day on Wednesday, 23 November 1977, gave the planners just three days to finalize all the details of what remained an almost reckless mission. Troops and aircrew and many of their aircraft had to be withdrawn from the field, equipped, briefed and moved into position on their starting positions by Tuesday, 22 November. The planners had the advantage of having on hand a corps of veteran, if youthful, Fireforce and Special Forces men with a wealth of battlefield experience and many low-level parachute descents behind them.

The first actions were to adopt the names '*Dingo*' (the overall title), 'Zulu 1' (the attack on Chimoio) and 'Zulu 2' (the Tembué phase), to confirm the choice of forward bases at Grand Reef and Lake Alexander, and the position of the administration base. The weather was studied, the sequences of airstrikes and para-drops were reviewed. Captain Jacques Dubois, second-in-command of the Mapping and Research section of the Rhodesian Intelligence Corps (RIC), was commissioned to build polystyrene and plaster of Paris target models over which he stretched the aerial photographs.

The details of the plan as presented to Ian Smith and the military hierarchy had been so carefully worked out that enough was ready on Sunday, 20 November, for the first of three briefings to be given in an aircraft hangar at New Sarum air force base.

In preparation for it and to allow everyone a clear vision of the briefers and their maps and diagrams, bleachers had been carried into the hangar from the New Sarum rugby ground and arranged along three sides of the large target model above which was suspended differently coloured circles indicated the flying patterns of the various types of aircraft.

At 1500hrs, Group Captain Norman Walsh briefed the air force commanders of the flying wings of New Sarum and Thornhill, the squadron and section leaders and the K-Car pilots. He gave them time to absorb the details portrayed on the target model, the accuracy of which had been confirmed by a captured ZANLA insurgent. One innovation was that prior to H-Hour, Captain Jack Malloch would fly his Douglas DC-8 cargo jet airliner at height over the ZANLA muster parades at New Farm at 0741hrs on a northeasterly bearing. It was intended that the roar of his four jet engines would mask any sound betrayed by the approaching armada of 58 aircraft and thereby prevent the camps being emptied before its arrival. It was hoped that, although startled by Malloch's engine noise, the ZANLA cadres would relax once they had spotted the aircraft, assuming it was a commercial flight bound for Malawi. Otherwise, the timings remained as planned. Diving from the west, three Hunters and four Vampires would strike the camp complex at 0745hrs (H-Hour), followed by the four Canberras 30 seconds later. Four more Hunters would join the initial three in suppressing anti-aircraft fire while, at 0747hrs (H+2 minutes), six Dakotas, each carrying 24 paratroops, flying in sections of three at 300–400 feet above the ground, would begin to drop their men along the southwestern and southeastern sides of the complex to form the two sides of the 'box'. Given the size of the complex, 25 square kilometres, the proposed rate of the drop at one man a second was designed to achieve a drop zone of three kilometres long, each zone receiving 72 paratroopers. This alone demonstrated the boldness of the plan, as there would be 42 metres between each man on landing, without any reserves behind him or the support of any heavy weapons. The troops had to win the fight with the weapons they were carrying. The third, northeastern, side would be established at 0750hrs (H+5 minutes) when the ten helicopters landed 40 2 Commando troopers behind a ridge running in the same direction. As these troops ran to occupy positions on the ridge, the ten K-Cars would climb to their optimum height of 800 feet and open fire on their preselected targets in an attempt to drive their inhabitants to ground. As they did, the command G-Car, piloted by Walsh, would orbit the battlefield, directing the air and ground attack. While the rest of the jet aircraft flew back to New Sarum, a 'cab-rank', a pair of Hunters, would orbit the target, ready for Walsh's call for airstrikes. A pair of Lynxes, one circling close in and the other farther out, would watch for any FPLM reaction from Chimoio and Vanduzi.

Back at New Sarum, the Canberras, Hunters and Vampires would be rearmed and refuelled. The fighters would then return in pairs to the target area. Three Canberras would be reloaded with Mk II Alpha bombs for possible restrikes on the camps. The fourth would be armed with 450kg bombs in case the FPLM bombarded Umtali in retaliation for the attack on Chimoio. The Canberra crews would remain at New Sarum on 'crew-room readiness'.

At 0800hrs (H+15 minutes), as two Vampire T11s armed with 60lb air-to-ground rockets took over the 'cab-rank' from the Hunters, the ten 'Polo' G-Cars were due at the admin area. The timing of their landing would allow Petter-Bowyer and his team to get ready to handle the arrival of 80 44-gallon drums of jet fuel, parachuted from Malloch's DC-7 cargo aircraft. The Support Commando mortar teams would unload their pair of 81mm mortar tubes and 100 bombs. Once they had set up a defensive position, some of them were to assist the technicians in carrying from the G-Cars ammunition trays of 4,400 20mm cannon shells for the K-Cars, boxes containing 7,500 rounds for the .303 Browning machine guns of the G-Cars and 20,000 7.62mm bullets to resupply the troops in the field. There were also demolition charges, medical equipment and the like to be unloaded. As soon as the DC-7 approached, a G-Car would mark the dropping zone with smoke and guide the large aircraft onto it. As the drums hit the ground, the team would roll them into position in lines to facilitate the multiple refuelling of arriving helicopters from the battlefield. Refuelled and rearmed K-Cars would fly back into action while the G-Cars would wait at the admin area, ready to evacuate any casualties and to supply any ammunition, water and other necessities as called for by the troops. Petter-Bowyer's air force technicians would stand by to repair any battle-damaged helicopters, the medical team would prepare to stabilize any casualties, and the SB element would await the arrival of any prisoners. The final task for his team was to assist in the afternoon withdrawal of parachutes, equipment and finally men by a helicopter shuttle via the admin area to Lake Alexander. From there, the SAS and Support Commando troops who were to parachute into Tembué would be driven to Grand Reef and flown back to New Sarum. The

Jack Malloch.
Photo: A Pride of Eagles

Major Jerry Strong.
Photo: The Saints

Captain Ian Buttenshaw.
Photo: The Saints

Major Nigel Henson.
Photo: Nigel Henson

CHAPTER SIX: THE BRIEFING FOR THE ATTCK ON NEW FARM, CHIMOIO

Captain Grahame Wilson.
Photo: PTS

Peter McAleese.
Photo: Graham Gillmore

Colour Sergeant John Norman.
Photo: RLIRA

Lieutenant Mark Adams.
Photo: RLIRA

helicopter fleet, carrying the designated protection troops and the paratrooper reserve from 2 and 3 Commandos, would fly cross-country to Mount Darwin in preparation for the next phase.

At 0900hrs on Monday, 21 November, Walsh and Major Robinson conducted a full briefing of the air and ground aspects of the attack to the air force, the SAS and RLI commanders of the units involved. They revealed that the overall commander, Lieutenant-General Peter Walls, commander of Combined Operations, would be flying in the command Dakota which was fitted out as a flying operations room with secure radio and teleprinters links to ComOps and the Prime Minister's Office. The aircraft would orbit close to the action to allow Walls to monitor the radio transmissions and take any needed strategic decisions. In direct tactical command, flying a specially modified command G-Car, would be Walsh, co-ordinating the air operations, and Robinson, directing the troops below him. Major Mick Graham, second-in-command of the SAS, was given command of the troops on the ground. His deputy would be Major Jeremy Strong BCR, the officer commanding of 3 Commando 1RLI. The command of the administration area to the north of New Farm was given to Group Captain Peter Petter-Bowyer and that of his protection troops to Captain Ian Buttenshaw, second-in-command of Support Commando 1RLI. Captain Peter Jackson of the SAS was put in charge of the helicopter assembly area at Lake Alexander. The officer commanding of Support Commando, Major Nigel Henson, would command the reserve formed by 48 of his paratroopers and stationed at Grand Reef airfield from where Dakotas could fly them into action if needed.

The troops selected for Zulu 1 were being withdrawn from their operational areas, as were the Dakotas, Lynxes and Alouettes from the various Fireforces. Commanded by Captain (later Lieutenant-Colonel) Grahame Wilson (destined to be Rhodesia's most decorated soldier), A Troop SAS was brought back from operations in Mozambique's Gaza Province to endure a long drive from Mabalauta near the southeastern border to Salisbury to join B Troop. On arrival they were told nothing more than to prepare their kit for parachuting. Peter McAleese, an ex-British paratrooper, thought the target was Malvernia. The 3 Commando troops believed it was a rumoured ZANLA camp of 300 men in the Zambezi Valley.

At 1300hrs on Tuesday, 22 November (D-Day minus 1), Robinson, Walsh, Captain Scott McCormack, the SAS intelligence officer, briefed their audience of 228 astounded men of the SAS, 3 and Support Commandos surrounding them on the bleachers. Missing were the 40 troops from 2 Commando, who were already at Grand Reef and who would be briefed separately.[3]

The briefers confined themselves to explaining the planned phases of Zulu 1 with reference to the model, their maps and gridded air photos, copies of the latter being supplied to every pilot and stick leader for use on the day.

Robinson explained that two 24-man 3 Commando stop groups, and one from the SAS, dropped slowly in a single line, would seal off the southwestern flank of the camp complex. Stop 1 would comprise twelve men from 3 Commando's 11 Troop, and twelve from 12 Troop, commanded by Colour Sergeant John Norman and Lieutenant Mark Adams respectively. Stop 2 likewise would be formed by twelve men from 13 Troop, commanded by Lieutenant John Cronin, and eleven from

Lieutenant John Cronin.
Photo: Tom Argyle

Captain Robert MacKenzie.
Source: Craig Fourie

Major Simon Haarhoff.
Photo: RLIRA

---

[3] Alexandre Binda, *The Saints: The Rhodesian Light Infantry*, 30° South Publishers, Johannesburg, 2007, p. 250.

Corporal Anthony Coom.
Photo: Tom Argyle

Mike McDonald.
Photo: Mike McDonald

Captain Cliff Webster.
Photo: A Pride of Eagles

Lieutenant-Colonel Peter Rich.
Photo: RLIRA

14 Troop plus Major Jeremy Strong, the officer commanding 3 Commando. Stop 3 would be Captain Colin Willis with 23 men of A Troop.

The southeastern flank would be covered by three SAS 24-man stop groups: Stop 4, Captain Robert MacKenzie and another 23 men from A Troop; Stop 5, 24 B Troop men including Lieutenant Ken Roberts and Major Mick Graham, the second-in-command; and Stop 6, Captain Grahame Wilson and 23 B Troop men.

The northwestern flank would be occupied by Stop A, Major Simon Haaroff's ten 2 Commando four-man helicopter-borne sticks.

Robinson described in exact detail what he expected from the troops, what they were to carry, their immediate actions on landing, their coalescing into sticks and the direction of the inward sweep, using fire and movement, and their objectives. He assigned to Major Henson's Support Commando the roles of the 81mm mortar crews at Lake Alexander and at the admin area, and its 48-man paratrooper reserve on standby at Grand Reef airstrip. Finally he revealed the withdrawal procedure.

Robinson told the paratroopers that they would exit their aircraft at their usual Fireforce altitude of 400–500 feet above ground. This was normal practice to minimize the time in the air under fire and to limit the possibility of drifting away from the dropping zone. This time, however, instead of dropping to confront an insurgent group of a dozen or so as they frequently did, they would be landing on the flanks of a vast sprawling complex containing somewhere between 9,000–11,000 trained and partly trained inhabitants with possibly half of them armed.

The familiar four-man stick would be retained within each 24-man stop group. They would wear their normal fighting kit which included a poncho or light sleeping bag, a tin or two of food, a sealed first aid dressing, a knife, spare radio batteries and the like. To avoid heat fatigue, they would take four instead of two one-litre water bottles. One member of the stick would have medical training and be equipped with a saline drip and a basic medical kit.

To avoid being mistaken for the enemy, the troops were ordered not to blacken their faces with camouflage cream as they would routinely do on Fireforce. For the same reason, only regulation Rhodesian webbing and camouflage uniforms were to be worn. In addition, Robinson had the troops sew plastic 'day-glo' orange patches inside their caps and to wear them inside out to make them visible to him and the pilots through the expected dense canopy of leaves. Fireforce troops were trained to attract the attention of pilots and Fireforce commanders by displaying the blank white back of a map or by heliograph.

Instead of carrying one VHF radio, the normal practice, the stick and stop group commanders would have two, one to be carried by one of their troopers. John Cronin (a Marine Corps Vietnam veteran), however, wore both radios for increased efficiency. The first radio was tuned to the battle or command net in order to communicate with Robinson and other stop groups and to call in airstrikes or for casualty evacuation, ammunition resupply and the like. The second radio would be tuned to the domestic channel of the stop group so as not to clutter up the command net. Robinson had the formidable task of handling the command net while listening to the exchanges on the seven domestic nets so that, if necessary, he could speak directly to individual stick commanders.

Most of the sticks would be armed with their FN rifles and MAG machine guns but some of the SAS machine-gunners would carry the lighter Soviet RPD and RPK machine guns. Firing the less powerful 7.62x39mm medium round, they ran the danger of being mistaken for the enemy but they knew from long experience they would also be able to replenish their belts and magazines from enemy stocks and casualties. To aid target marking, Robinson ordered all riflemen to load one tracer after every fifth ball round. The paratroopers also armed themselves with 9mm-calibre pistols, secured by lanyards. They did so for self-protection if their parachutes were snagged and left them hanging high in the trees and they could not free the rifles or machine guns strapped to their bodies. Two of the riflemen would equip themselves with both the 42Z anti-armour and phosphorus rifle grenades.

Each rifleman would have to find room for twelve spare FN magazines (260 rounds including the magazine on his rifle), a 100-round MAG or RPD belt, flares and four high-explosive or phosphorus grenades. The stick commander might not carry a spare MAG belt but he would be burdened by all the rest plus the radio, radio codes, maps, compass, protractor and the gridded air photo. The MAG/RPD gunner would be weighed down by ten 50-round belts and two grenades aside from his kit. If this

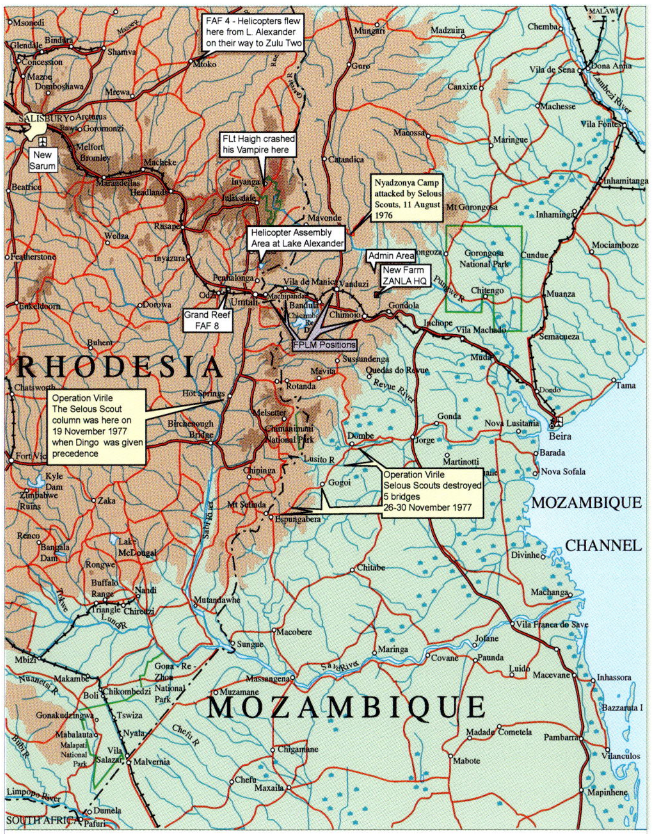

Heights above Sea Level
= 2 500 metres
= 2 000
= 1 500
= 1 000
= 500

Operation Dingo, Zulu 1
The Attack on the ZANLA Camp at New Farm, Chimoio
Wednesday, 23 November 1977

0 20 40 60 80 100 120 140 160 180 200 220 240 260 280 300 kilometres

J.R.T. Wood

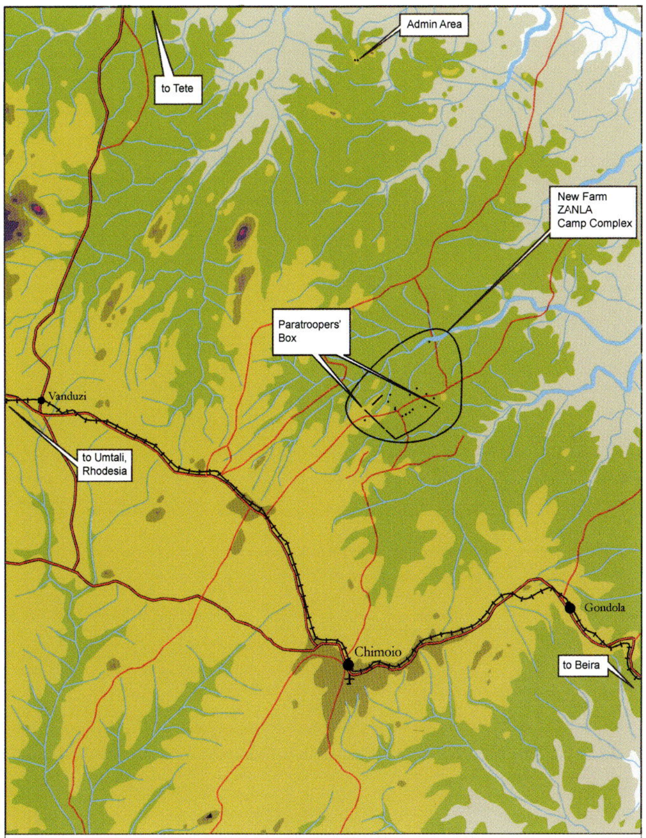

= 900 metres
= 800 metres
= 700 metres
= 600 metres
= 500 metres
= 400 metres
= 300 metres
= 200 metres

Operation Dingo, Zulu 1
The Attack on the ZANLA Camp at New Farm, Chimoio
Wednesday, 23 November 1977

0 5 10 15 20
kilometres

J.R.T. Wood

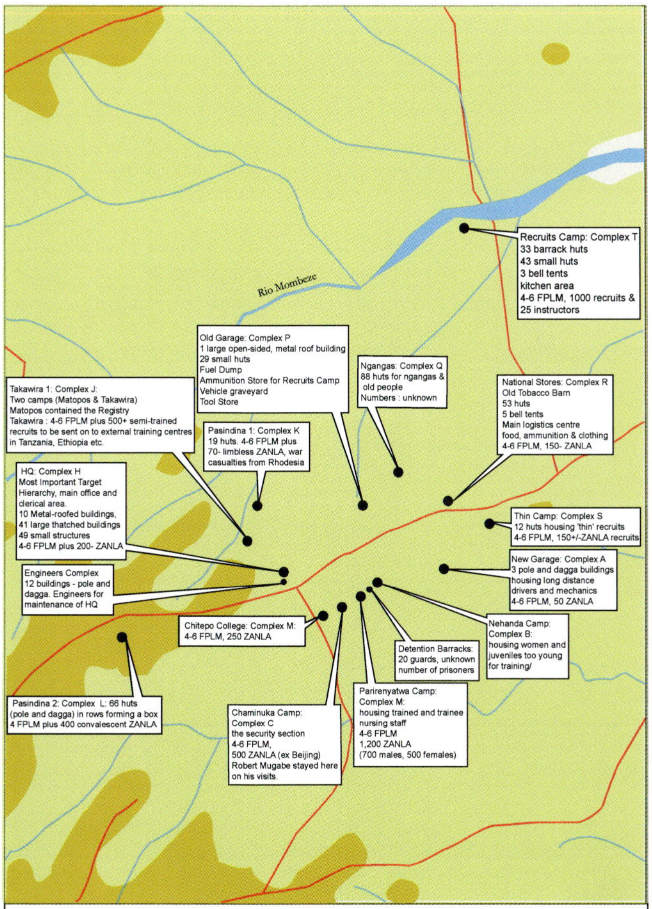

New Farm
ZANLA Complex of Camps

0 1 2 3 4 5 6
Kilometres

J.R.T. Wood

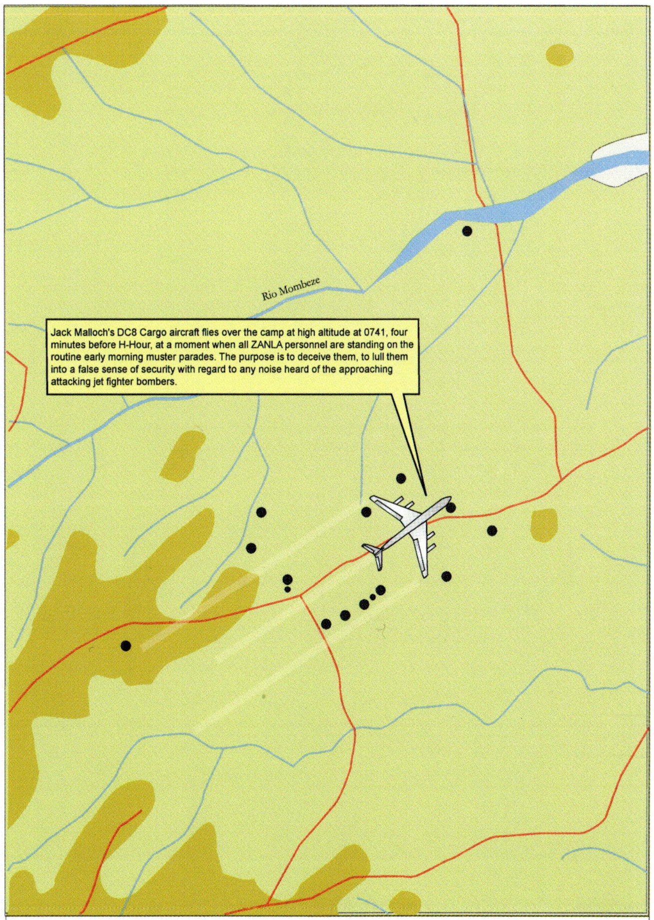

Operation Dingo
Zulu 1
Deception at Chimoio at H-4 minutes

0 1 2 3 4 5 6
Kilometres

J.R.T. Wood

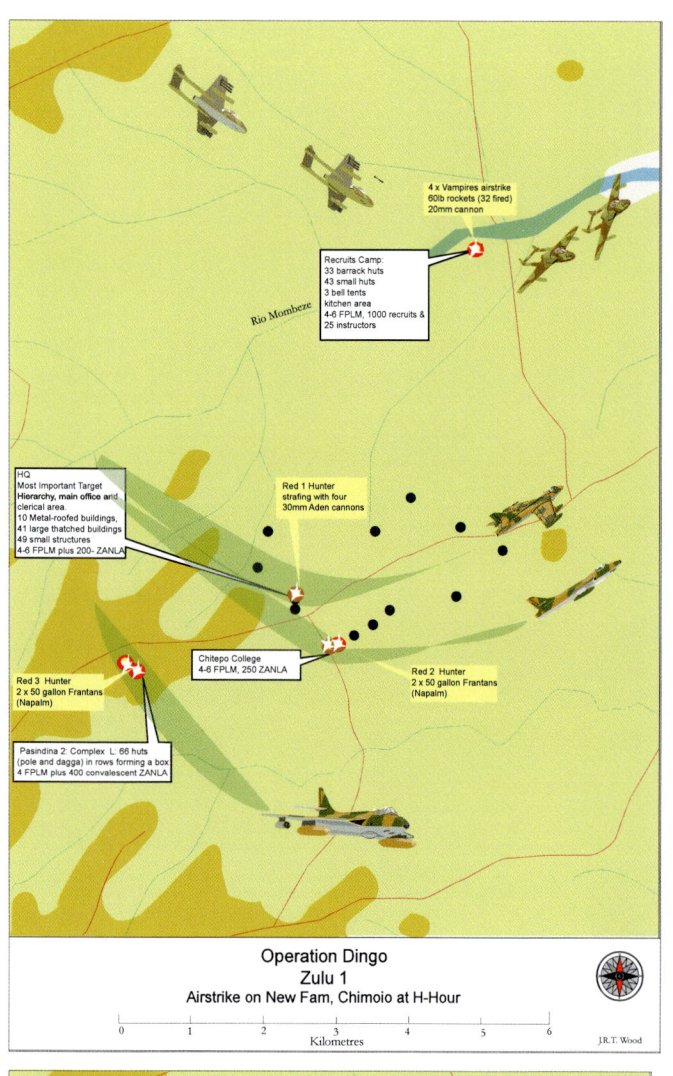

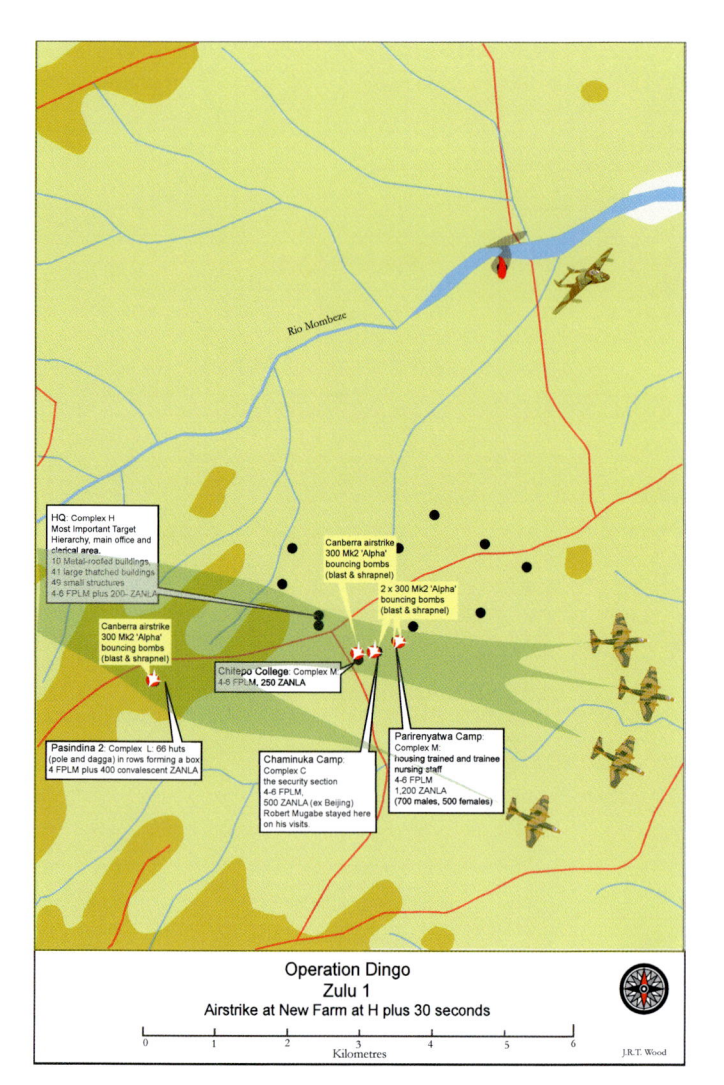

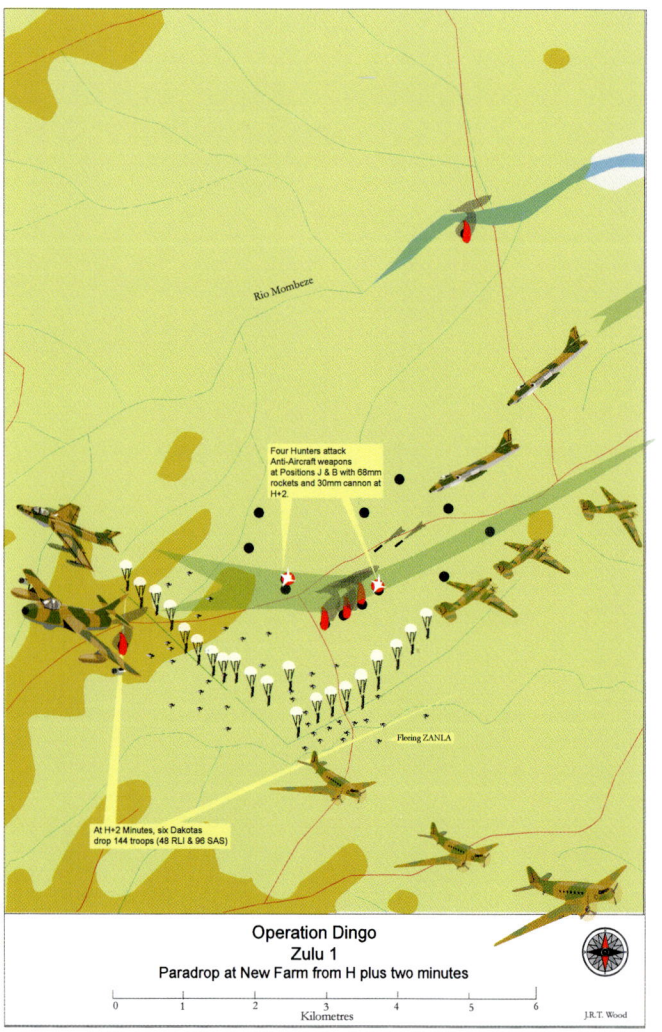

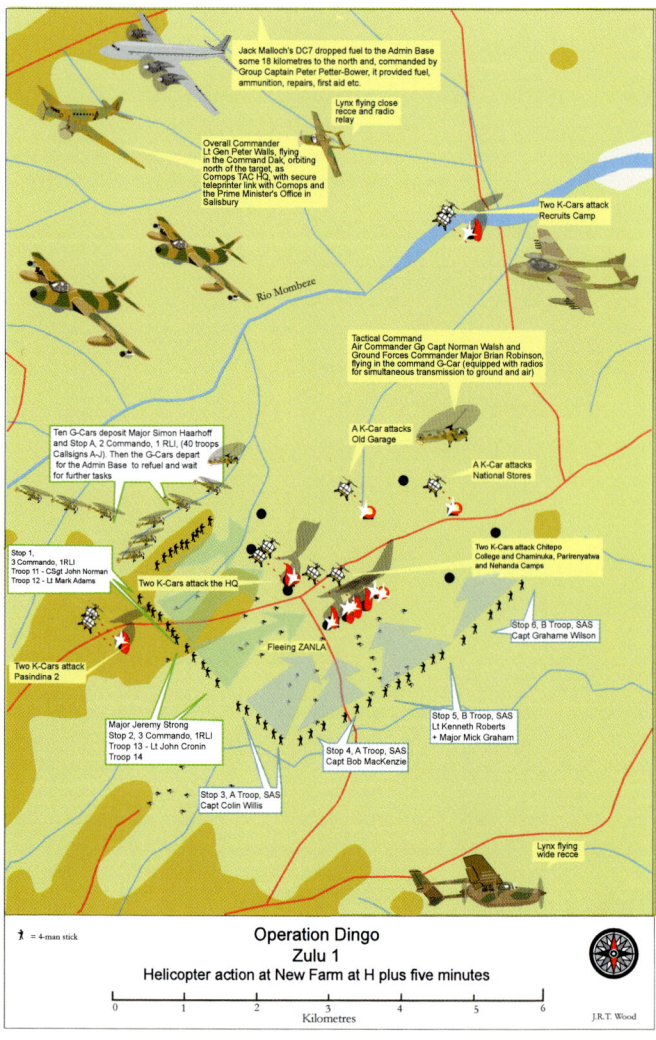

AFRICA@WAR VOLUME I: OPERATION DINGO—RHODESIAN RAID ON CHIMOIO AND TEMBUÉ, 1977

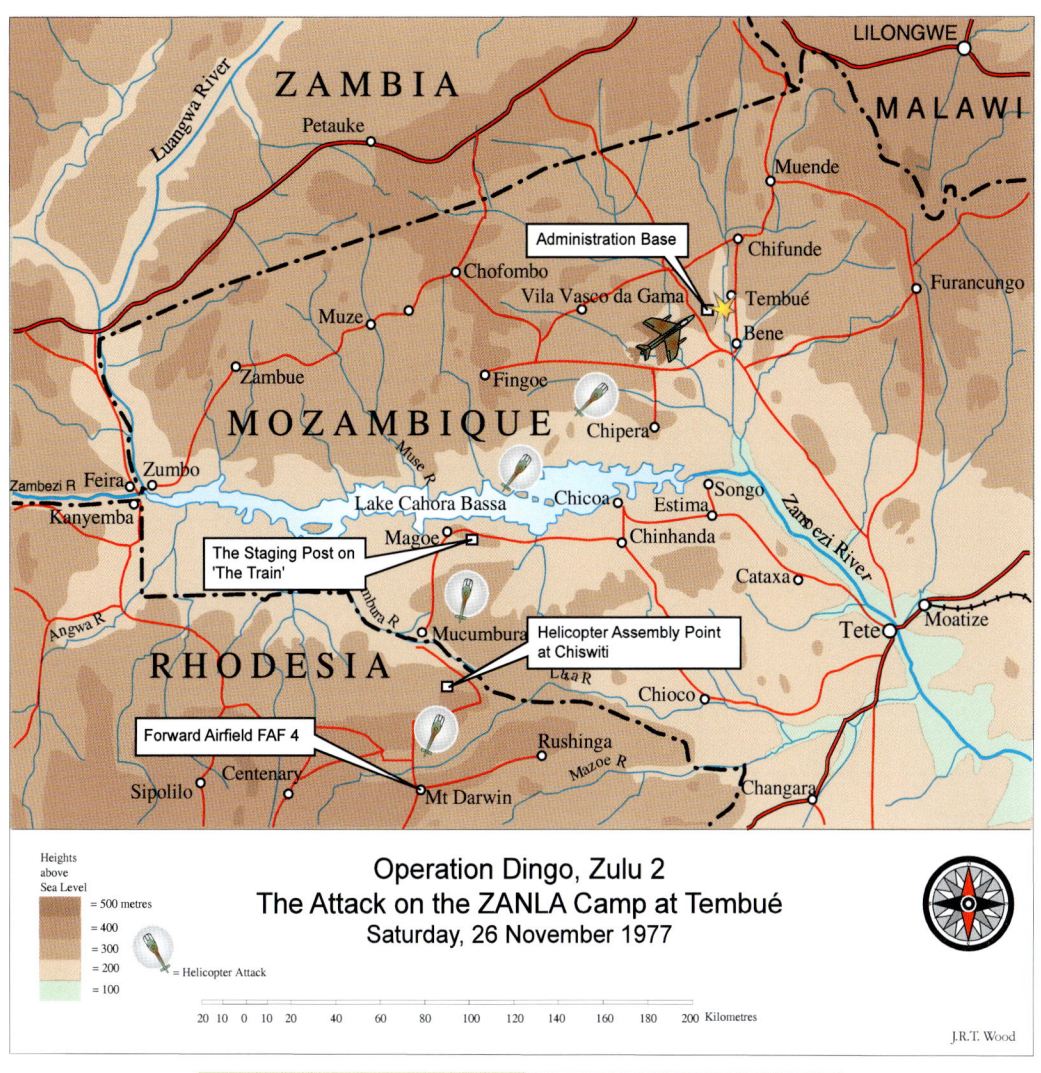

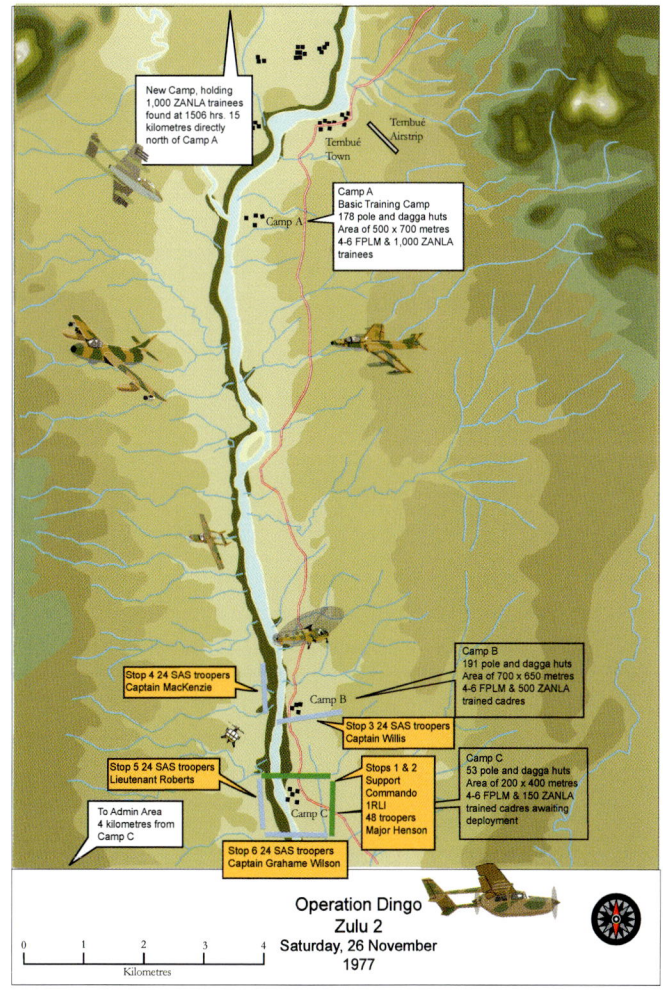

Operation Dingo, Zulu 2
The Attack on the ZANLA Camp at Tembué
Saturday, 26 November 1977

Operation Dingo
Zulu 2
Saturday, 26 November 1977

AFRICA@WAR VOLUME I: OPERATION DINGO—RHODESIAN RAID ON CHIMOIO AND TEMBUÉ, 1977

Weight 42 kg
Length 1.76 metre
Cartridge 20 x 82 mm cartridge
Calibre 20 mm
Rate of fire 600-750 rpm
Muzzle velocity 720 m/s

Matra MG151 20mm cannon

Browning Mk II .303in calibre machine-gun

Calibre: 0.303in
Weight: 21 lb 14 oz
Muzzle velocity: 2,660 ft/sec
Rate of fire: 1,150 rpm
Maximum Range: 3,000 ft
Length: 3 ft 8.5 in

AK-47 (Avtomat Kalashnikova) Assault Rifle

Calibre: 7.62mm.
Cartridge: 7.62 x 39mm.
Weight: 4.3kg (9.5 lb).
Length: 870mm (34.3 in).
Muzzle velocity: 715m/sec (2,346 ft/sec).
Rate of fire: 600 rpm.
Effective Range: 300m (on automatic) - 400 metres (semi-automatic).
Feed System: 30 or 40 round detachable box magazine.

FN FAL (Fusil Automatique Léger) Rifle

Calibre: 7.62mm.
Cartridge: 7.62 x 51mm NATO.
Weight: 4.3kg (9.5 lb).
Length: 1,090mm (42.9 in).
Muzzle velocity: 840m/sec (2,756 ft/sec).
Rate of fire: 650 rpm.
Effective Range: 600m.
Feed System: 30 round detachable box magazine.

MAG General Purpose Machine-Gun

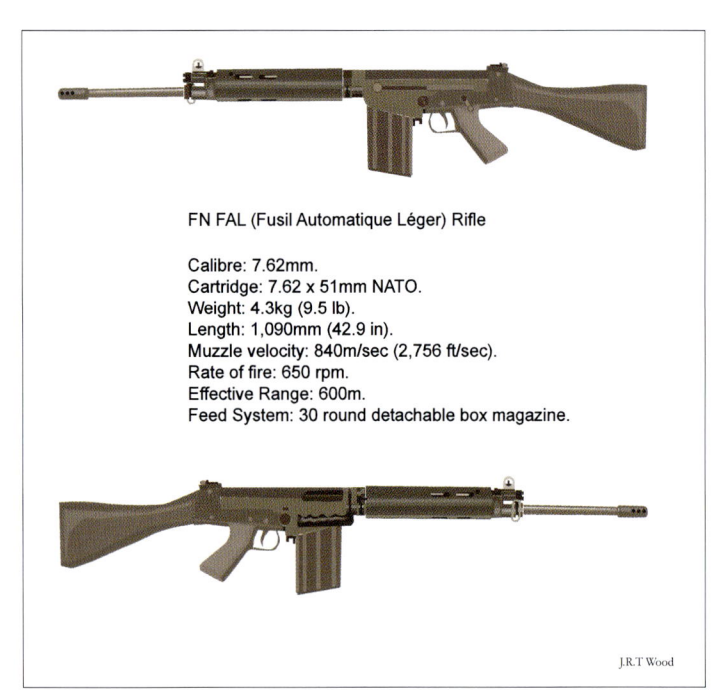

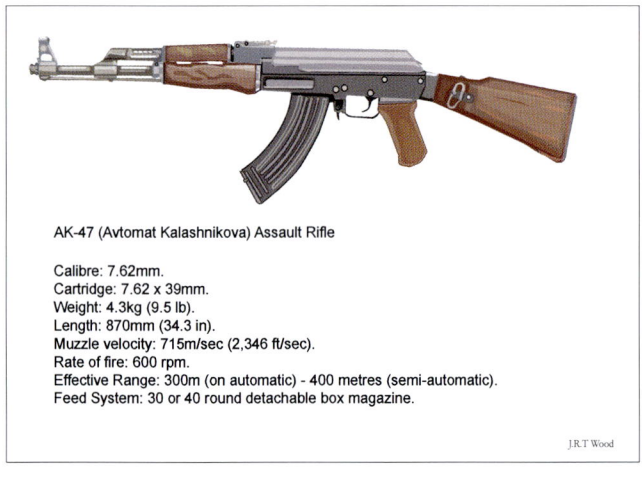

Weight: 11.79 kg (25.99 lb)
Length: 1,263 mm (49.7 in)
Barrel length: 630 mm (24.8 in)
Width: 118.7 mm (4.7 in)
Height: 263 mm (10.4 in)
Cartridge: 7.62×51mm NATO
Action: Gas-operated, open bolt
Rate of fire: 650–1,000 rounds/min
Muzzle velocity: 840 m/s (2,756 ft/s)
Effective range: 800 metres
Maximum range: 1,500 m from tripod
Feed system: Non-disintegrating DM1 or disintegrating M13 linked belt
Sights: Folding leaf sight with aperture and notch, front blade

The 'Pookie': groundbreaking Rhodesian-designed and -manufactured landmine detection vehicle. *Source: J.R.T. Wood*

Operation *Hurricane*. A painting of a Fireforce action on a farm in the Centenary district.
Source: Craig Bone

Combined early operations in the Zambezi valley with the RLI, BSAP and National Parks personnel showing off captured guerrilla weapons. *Photo: The Saints*

The all-important Fireforce third wave or 'land tail'.
Photos: Claude Botha (top pair) and Tom Argyle

A Camberra bomber in flight.
Photo: A Pride of Eagles

Hawker Hunter fighter jet.
Photo: A Pride of Eagles

G-Car.
Source: J.R.T. Wood

The C-47 'Dakota', military workhorse since the Second World War.
Photo: A Pride of Eagles

Reims Cessna 'Lynx' ground-attack aircraft, a formidable weapon of war. *Photo: Tom Argyle*

Lynx take-off.
Photo: The Saints

Lynx strike in a riverbed.
Photo: The Saints

ZANLA prisoners being loaded onto an Alouette G-car.
Photo: Max T

An Alouette gunner-technician checks for obstacles on touchdown.
Photo: Max T

A Vampire takes off.
Photo: The Saints

A Lynx frantam / napalm strike.
Photo: The Saints

RLI paratroopers inside a Dakota ready to jump.
Photo: The Saints

Paras ready to emplane, Corporal Charlie Warren, 3 Commando, does some last-minute equipment checks. *Photo: Claude Botha*

An RLI trooper checks out a guerrilla camp in enemy territory, prior to an assault.
Photo: Max T

82mm mortar.
Photo: Tom Argyle

Corporal Fraser Brown, 2 Commando RLI, mans an observation post in hostile country.
Photo: Fraser Brown

3 Commando paratroopers, Trooper Alex Nicholl, Sergeant Tony Coom and Trooper Jerry Stander, prior to an 'external'. *Photo: Tom Argyle*

3 Commando paras take five in a ZANLA buildlng after the assault on Chimoio.
Photo: RLIRA

were not a formidable enough weight to bear, Captain Robert MacKenzie (a US Army Vietnam veteran) had his men carry 600 rifle rounds and his RPD gunners 1,500 rounds.[4] MacKenzie armed himself with a Colt AR-15, firing the 5.56mm (.223in) high-velocity round.

Robinson reminded the paratroopers that their first actions on landing were to rid themselves of their parachute harness, make contact with the nearest man, take cover, watch and shoot. Immediately thereafter, the men had to form up in their sticks and therefore in their stop groups. The stop commander would position himself in the middle of the aircraft so that he would land in the middle of his zone enabling his men to look inward for his directions. The men at either end of the stop group would throw white phosphorus grenades to mark the FLOT (front line of troops) for the orbiting aircraft and the command helicopter in particular.

Before any movement forward, Robinson ordered that each man would take note of where he had left his parachute and jump helmet. This was because international sanctions made parachutes expensive and difficult to obtain. At the end of the day, the first duty of the troopers would be to recover their parachutes to be removed by the G-Cars as a first load for repacking at New Sarum for use on Zulu 2.

McAleese found Robinson's briefing "the finest ops brief I have ever heard. He was a small, wiry terrier of a man who was the driving force behind the success of the Rhodesian SAS and he really wound us up for the fight that day".[5] The 29 year-old Corporal Anthony Harold Coom of 12 Troop 3 Commando, however, recalls having the reverse reaction. The more confident the "rather gung-ho" Robinson sounded, the more Coom's stomach churned "at the thought of the odds and the task at hand". He conceded that "this Boys' Own stuff was not really my strong point and in my opinion best left to those who found war appealing".[6] Mike McDonald, a Canadian MAG gunner in 3 Commando, counted the figures given for each of the camps and arrived at a total of 5,000 ZANLA cadres to be faced. The odds against success appeared so fearsome that the joke in the RLI ranks was this could be 'A *Gomo* [hill] Too Far' (a play on the title of the 1977 film 'A Bridge Too Far' based on Cornelius Ryan's book on the ill-fated attack on Arnhem in 1944).[7]

The meeting broke for tea. When it reassembled, Robinson briefed it on the aims and details of Zulu 2, the Tembué attack. He closed by wishing the RLI "good luck", and adding light-heartedly that the SAS as "professionals don't need it". Or so McAleese recalls.[8] John Cronin by contrast remembered Robinson wishing them all good luck before General Walls made a short closing speech.[9]

Immediately afterward, a convoy departed for Grand Reef, Umtali, 200 kilometres away. It carried three teams from Support Commando: Major Henson and his 47 reserve paratroopers, the 20 men and their four 81mm mortars and Captain Ian Buttenshaw, his second-in-command, and his 15 troops and their two 81mm mortars allocated respectively to the protection of the helicopter assembly area at Lake Alexander and the admin area north of New Farm, Chimoio. Also aboard the convoy were Captain Cliff Webster, the RLI doctor, and four medical orderlies (to provide resuscitation and first aid to casualties arriving at the admin area, Lake Alexander and Grand Reef), four members of the Special Branch, and a quartermaster to set up a supply point at Grand Reef.

Four Lynxes flew into Grand Reef before dusk. The convoy from New Sarum would arrive some hours later. Already there a couple of days earlier were Major Simon Haaroff of 2 Commando and his 38 men who would constitute Stop A, the helicopter-borne troops. They had endured a long drive across the breadth of Rhodesia, from the far northwest Victoria Falls area via Bulawayo. Since then they had undergone intensive training, briefing and final preparations for the attack. Their number would be made up to 40 shortly by the arrival of Lieutenant-Colonel Peter Rich, the commanding officer of the RLI, who had decided not to miss the action. He chose to be Haaroff's radioman for the day. The 51-year-old Peter Rich was a veteran of two other conflicts, having fought in the Korean War as a platoon commander in the Norfolk Regiment and in Malaya with 22 SAS.

At 1800hrs four Vampire FB9s and two T11s of No. 2 Squadron landed at New Sarum where the SAS and 3 Commando paratroopers had completed their individual unit briefings, had revised their drills, assigned their tasks and were preparing their kit and weapons for their drop in a 'hot DZ' the next day.

Sleep would not come easily that hot night to the young men of *Dingo* at New Sarum, Thornhill and Grand Reef, given the enormity of their task ahead.

---

[4] Robert MacKenzie, 'Fast Strike on Chimoio II', *Soldier of Fortune*, February '94, pp. 41–43 & 83–84.

[5] Peter McAleese, *No Mean Soldier*, Orion, London, 1993, pp. 129–132.

[6] Binda, p. 258.

[7] www.therli.com, Mike McDonald, Operation *Dingo*, November 1977.

[8] McAleese, p. 132.

[9] Memorandum by Maj John R. Cronin, 23–24 February 1998.

CHAPTER SEVEN:
ZULU 1: THE ATTACK ON NEW FARM, CHIMOIO, WEDNESDAY, 23–24 NOVEMBER 1977

Zulu 1, the first phase of Operation *Dingo*, began quietly at 0300hrs on Wednesday, 23 November 1977, when the SAS and 3 Commando paratroops and the 2 Commando and the Support Commando troopers were awakened at New Sarum and Grand Reef. The task before them would take longer than the planners envisaged. Even so, they were to create a template for the 30 or more external operations that would be mounted until the ceasefire in 1980.

The paratroopers drew their parachutes and paired off for mutual support; each man checked his partner's kit and tightened his straps. The men at Grand Reef donned their kit, picked up their weapons and boarded their vehicles for the drive to Lake Alexander, 40 kilometres north of Umtali, close to the Mozambican border. The convoy was carrying drums of aviation fuel to refuel the helicopters. Staying behind were Major Nigel Henson and his Support Commando paratrooper reserve, waiting for a possible Dakota flight into action later in the day.

At 0430hrs, with first faint streaks of dawn defining the horizon at New Sarum, Air Marshal Frank Mussell, commander of the air force, saw off the departure of the 31 Alouette III helicopters, flying off in waves of five. They were led by Squadron Leader Harold Griffiths, the officer commanding No. 7 (Helicopter) Squadron and included ten K-Cars, ten Rhodesian and ten South African 'Polo' G-Cars and the specially equipped command G-Car, flown by Group Captain Norman Walsh with Major Brian Robinson seated next to him.

At 0600hrs, Flight Lieutenant Bob d'Hotman, leading the six Dakotas with full loads of 24 paratroopers each and the command Dakota carrying General Walls, roared down the long runway at New Sarum.

With the helicopters due at Lake Alexander at 0630hrs, the personnel there were rolling 31 fuel drums into separate positions to facilitate a quick refuelling. That done the 20 men of Support Commando set up their 81mm mortar tubes to protect the landing. Everything was going to plan except the weather. The mountains were shrouded in thick cloud and beyond them the cloud ceiling was down to 300 feet above the Mozambican plain. One result was that at Thornhill the armament of the initial wave of Hunters was changed from Golf bombs to frantan (napalm) because of the cloud cover. For safety reasons, the Golf required to be released at 4,500 feet above ground after a 60-degree high-dive profile. Frantan, by contrast, would be delivered at low level.

Having picked up Major Haaroff's men, including Lieutenant-Colonel Rich, the ten Rhodesian G-Cars and the command helicopter followed the K-Cars back into the air at 0710hrs bound for New Farm, Chimoio. Squadron Leader Griffiths, leading, found the route he had chosen blocked by cloud. With any delay affecting his expected time of arrival, Griffiths searched and then found a clear valley down which he led the fleet. Once under the cloud, the helicopters dropped down to treetop level, to present as fleeting a target as possible and to diminish the noise of their engines.

D'Hotman's six Dakotas passed Griffiths in the clouds above. The command Dakota broke away, heading for its orbiting point 23 kilometres north of New Farm. Higher above the cloud flew the formations of seven Hunters, four Vampire FB9s and four Canberras. As H-Hour approached, three of the Hunters and the Vampires accelerated ahead.

0741–0815hrs (H-4 to H+45 minutes)

At 0741hrs, however, cloud cover over the target was broken enough for the opening ruse to work. Suddenly climbing to create maximum noise from its four jet engines, the Afretair Douglas DC-8 cargo liner roared overhead, alarming and scattering the muster parades in the camps. The

Air Marshal Frank Mussell.
Photo: A Pride of Eagles

Air Lieutenant David Bourhill.
Photo: A Pride of Eagles

Squadron Leader Steve Kesby.
Photo: A Pride of Eagles

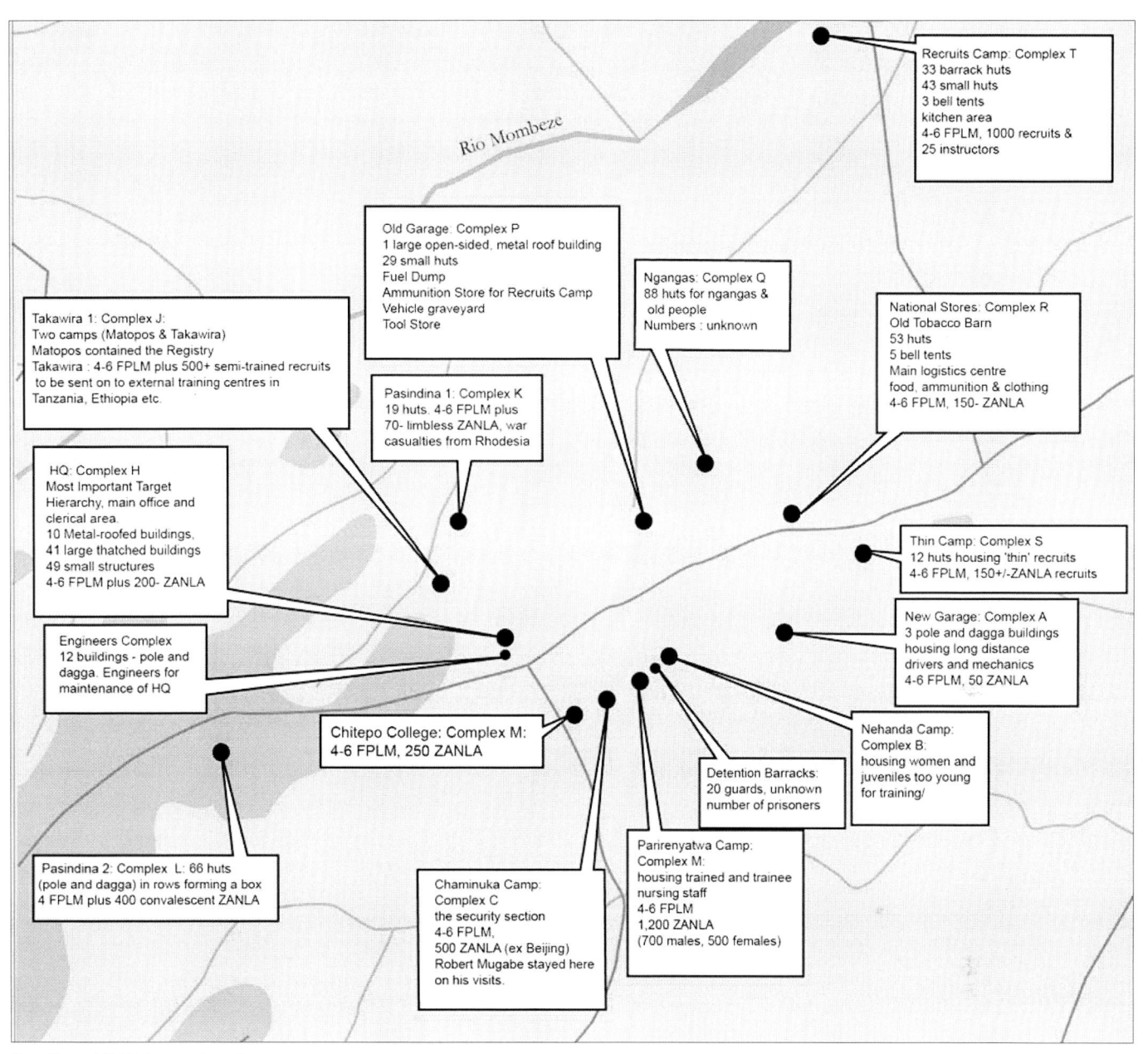

CHAPTER SEVEN: ZULU1: THE ATTACK ON NEW FARM CHIMOIO, 23–24 NOVEMBER 1977

Recruits Camp: Complex T
33 barrack huts
43 small huts
3 bell tents
kitchen area
4-6 FPLM, 1000 recruits &
25 instructors

Rio Mombeze

Old Garage: Complex P
1 large open-sided, metal roof building
29 small huts
Fuel Dump
Ammunition Store for Recruits Camp
Vehicle graveyard
Tool Store

Ngangas: Complex Q
88 huts for ngangas &
old people
Numbers : unknown

National Stores: Complex R
Old Tobacco Barn
53 huts
5 bell tents
Main logistics centre
food, ammunition & clothing
4-6 FPLM, 150- ZANLA

Takawira 1: Complex J:
Two camps (Matopos & Takawira)
Matopos contained the Registry
Takawira : 4-6 FPLM plus 500+ semi-trained recruits
to be sent on to external training centres in
Tanzania, Ethiopia etc.

Pasindina 1: Complex K
19 huts. 4-6 FPLM plus
70- limbless ZANLA, war
casualties from Rhodesia

HQ: Complex H
Most Important Target
Hierarchy, main office and
clerical area.
10 Metal-roofed buildings,
41 large thatched buildings
49 small structures
4-6 FPLM plus 200- ZANLA

Thin Camp: Complex S
12 huts housing 'thin' recruits
4-6 FPLM, 150+/-ZANLA recruits

Engineers Complex
12 buildings - pole and
dagga. Engineers for
maintenance of HQ

New Garage: Complex A
3 pole and dagga buildings
housing long distance
drivers and mechanics
4-6 FPLM, 50 ZANLA

Chitepo College: Complex M:
4-6 FPLM, 250 ZANLA

**Nehanda Camp:
Complex B:**
housing women and
juveniles too young
for training/

Detention Barracks:
20 guards, unknown
number of prisoners

Pasindina 2: Complex L: 66 huts
(pole and dagga) in rows forming a box
4 FPLM plus 400 convalescent ZANLA

**Chaminuka Camp:
Complex C**
the security section
4-6 FPLM,
500 ZANLA (ex Beijing)
Robert Mugabe stayed here
on his visits.

**Parirenyatwa Camp:
Complex M:**
housing trained and trainee
nursing staff
4-6 FPLM
1,200 ZANLA
(700 males, 500 females)

New Farm ZANLA complex of camps.
Source: J.R.T. Wood

ZANLA muster parades reformed as the DC-8 rumbled away northeastward.

At 0745hrs (H-Hour), flying in line abreast, three Hunters of Red Section attacked New Farm. Red 1, Squadron Leader Richard Brand (the officer commanding No. 1 (Hunter) Squadron) opened Operation *Dingo* with a long burst of fire from his four 30mm Aden cannons. Diving, he strafed the sprawling ZANLA headquarters—the former farmhouse, nine corrugated-iron-roofed outhouses and the surrounding 41 thatched buildings and 49 pole and mud huts. On his left across the road, Red 2, Air Lieutenant David Bourhill, dropped a pair of 50-gallon frantan bombs on Chitepo College which housed 250 ZANLA trainees and staff. He followed Brand up into an orbit.

The right-hand Hunter, Red 3, flown by Squadron Leader John Annan, hit the westernmost camp, Pasindina 2, with his frantan bombs, setting alight many of its 66 thatched huts. Pasindina 2 was home to 400 veteran ZANLA convalescents, recovering from wounds and illnesses contracted while on operations in Rhodesia. Annan then raked huts along the tree line to the north of the camp with his cannons before climbing to rejoin the other two.

As Red Section turned in to restrike, the fires they had initiated belched fireballs, blown upward by fierce convection currents, marking the camps for the fast-approaching Canberra bombers beneath them.[10]

Flying at 350 knots at 300 feet above the ground, their optimum bombing profile, the Canberras headed for their selected targets. The leading Canberra overshot Pasindina 2 slightly and ran a full load of 300 bouncing, exploding 155mm spherical Alpha bombs through the second half of the burning camp and beyond. The second Canberra deluged the headquarters complex with its Alphas, killing 600 ZANLA personnel. The two following

---

[10] British Empire and Commonwealth Museum, Rhodesian Army Association Papers, Box 844, Airstrike Report, 23 November 1977.

Hunter in flight.
Photo: A Pride of Eagles

A pair of Vampires in flight.
Photo: A Pride of Eagles

Three C-47s in flight, doors open and dispatchers at the ready.
Photo: The Saints

Canberras smothered Chitepo College and its immediate neighbours, Chaminuka Camp (housing the ZANLA security section and 500 Peking-trained insurgents, and where Mugabe stayed on his visits) and Parirenyatwa Camp (inhabited by 1,200 male and female trained and trainee nursing staff). The four Canberras turned away, heading for New Sarum to refuel and rearm with Alpha bombs. Events at Chimoio, however, meant they were not held there on 'crew-room readiness' but would return to join the cab-rank, flying at 15,000 feet above the target.

The 1,000 recruits, 25 instructors and six FPLM soldiers mustering at the Recruits' Camp (made up of 33 barrack huts, 43 thatched huts and three bell tents), five kilometres to the north, had also been caught on muster parade at H-Hour. Four diving Vampire FB9s loosed at them a barrage of 36 60lb 'squash head' high-explosive rockets and strafed them with their four 20mm Hispano cannons. Squadron Leader Steve Kesby noticed the startled flight of the men in front of him as he fired his eight rockets.[11]

As the Canberras had cleared the area, Red Section returned to attack fresh targets. Red 1 fired a ripple of 68mm Matra high-explosive rockets at ZANLA's main logistics centre, the National Stores, holding the complex's food, clothing and ammunition. Encircled by a bulldozed firebreak, National Stores comprised a former tobacco barn, surrounded by 53 huts and five bell tents and housed 150 ZANLA personnel. Red 1 then rocketed and strafed the Old Garage. Red 2 followed him firing his cannons at both targets. Red 3 returned to the huts along the tree line north of Pasindina 2 to give them another dose of 30mm cannon shells. He climbed again to join the rest of Red Section to form the first cab-rank of the day.

On time, at 0747hrs (H+2 minutes), the two sections of three Dakotas each approached their drop zones, flying at 500 feet above the ground.

The initial shock was over. Despite the crippling casualties, the ZANLA anti-aircraft gun crews began to fight back, which was anticipated; two pairs of Hunters, Blue and White Sections, dived in to suppress any fire directed at the slow Dakotas and their vulnerable cargoes of parachutists. They attacked the gun pits, as well as the camps that had escaped attention in the initial airstrike, with 68mm Matra rockets and 30mm cannon shells.

Expending 40 rockets and 500 shells, White Section (Vic Wightman, White 1, and Spook Geraty, White 2) attacked two of the anti-aircraft sites and set the huts at Takawira Camp alight. Takawira and its neighbour, Matopos Camp which housed the registry, formed a two-camp complex 500 metres northeast of the headquarters and held 500 semi-trained recruits due to go for further training in Tanzania, Ethiopia and elsewhere. The ZANLA gunners, however, responded with long bursts of green and red tracer. A bullet from gun pit 2 holed Wightman's aircraft above its port engine intake.

Flying to the right of White Section, Flight Lieutenant J.R. Blythewood, Blue 1, fired 24 Matra rockets into gun pit 2 and

---

[11] Beryl Salt, *A Pride of Eagles: The Definitive History of the Rhodesian Air Force: 1920–1980*, Covos Day, Weltevreden Park, 2001, p. 595.

From the open door of a Dakota, another Dakota carrying paratroopers en route to Chimoio.
Photo: Pete MacDonald

"Green light on! ... Go ... go ... go ..."
Photo: Tom Argyle

with his 30mm cannons collapsed the tents in Nehanda Camp, the eastern neighbour of the already stricken Parirenyatwa medical camp. Then he fired 16 rockets at the National Stores complex, adding a burst of 30mm fire. Blue 2, Air Lieutenant Martin Lowrie, strafed gun pit 4 with his 30mm cannons and then, ordered by the arriving Group Captain Walsh, fired his 68mm rockets at the mill at National Stores.

Above this action, two Vampire T11s, each armed with eight 60lb rockets and their four 20mm guns and one flown by Group Captain F.D. 'Tol' Janeke, reinforced Red Section's Hunters in the cab-rank.

The anti-aircraft gunners aside, most of the ZANLA personnel were scattering. One recalled, "Within seconds planes were moving about in the air and we were all scared. We couldn't think what to do except to run. I rolled and rolled across the ground and hid under a bush. Then a bomb dropped on the spot where I had just been. I rolled again and fell into a pit and broke my arm. I had to leave my gun. Now people were running in all directions."[12] A female survivor, Olaria Lucia Chikuhuhu, muddied her clothes to dull their bright colours and started to walk out of the complex, "passing through many sub-bases with a lot of dead bodies of my fellow comrades. I couldn't control my tears. When I looked in every direction I saw a Daicotar [Dakota] deploying ground forces." Covering herself with blood, she lay among the bodies feigning death. Later the Rhodesian troops kicked her as they examined the corpses but she did not give herself away. Later a grass fire burned toward where she lay but she managed to get away unseen.[13]

The tracer fire spitting at them through the billowing smoke from the burning camps, failed to distract the six Dakota pilots as they flew their aircraft, steadily maintaining an altitude of 450 feet above ground, along their allotted sections of the dropping zone, disgorging paratroopers. Almost as they opened, the dull green parachutes floated rapidly down into the trees.

SAS Captain Robert MacKenzie, waiting to jump, noted an increasing volume of flak as his aircraft approached the dropping zone. Peter McAleese watched a Vampire T11 dive in to suppress it. Mike McDonald, the RLI MAG gunner, remembers there was a "huge fireball over the main camp" and the sound of constant gunfire.[14] To Corporal Peter Leid, the 3 Commando medic: "It was awesome seeing the long 'J' curve of parachutes in the sky,

---

[12] Dudley Cowderoy & Roy Nesbit, *War in the Air: Rhodesian Air Force 1935–1980*, Galago, Alberton, 1987, p. 82.

[13] David Caute, *Under the Skin: The Death of White Rhodesia,* Allen Lane, London, 1982, pp. 140–141.

[14] McDonald.

Vic Wightman.
Photo: A Pride of Eagles

"... parachutes floated down rapidly ..."

Paratroopers await the instruction to "Stand up, hook up, check equipment!" *Photo: The Saints*

Paratroopers descend.
Photo: Giles Gillespie

a thing of rare beauty."[15] Glancing down as he leaped clear of his aircraft, McAleese saw a mass of running figures, some firing weapons over their shoulders. He blessed ZANLA's poor fire discipline. The main ZANLA escape route was southeast through the cordon being formed by the 3 Commando Stops 1 and 2 and the SAS Stops 3 and 4. With his parachute snagged by two trees, Stop 3's commander, Captain Colin Willis, faced ten ZANLA men charging at him. He drew his pistol and knocked one down beneath him. Coming to his aid, SAS Sergeant Les Clarke accounted for six more. Willis swung himself to the nearest tree and climbed down it.[16] The commander of Stop 4, MacKenzie, snagged a mopane tree on his way down, which jerked him to a stop six inches above the ground. He hit his quick release and ducked behind a tree.[17] McAleese was also caught up in a tree, a few feet above a large termite mound. Fired at by a ZANLA cadre from behind a tree, he tugged the capewell releases at his shoulders and slid down the anthill still wearing his parachute harness. He unstrapped his RPK machine gun and he and his partner, Steve Kluzniak, also armed with an RPK, returned fire. Out of ammunition, the ZANLA gunman tried to surrender but was gunned down.[18] Nearby a stick of four opened fire and killed 80 of the men running at them.[19]

To the left of Willis and MacKenzie, Charlie Warren of Stop 2 and his MAG gunner, Keith White, were still in the air when they came under fire from a dozen ZANLA cadres running at them. Warren drew and returned fire with his 9mm pistol. This distracted him and he did not have time to adopt the correct flex-kneed stance before hitting the ground hard. Winded, sucking for breath, he pulled his rifle free of his parachute harness and, still under fire, dived into cover. From there, he opened fire on a group running 200 metres to his front. He and White then linked up with Major Jeremy Strong, their 3 Commando officer commanding.[20]

Although he landed safely, Mike McDonald's parachute, snagged in a small tree, became the target for considerable fire from a bushy streambank 70 metres away across intervening flat open ground.[21]

By contrast, Stop 1, the first down, had enjoyed a peaceful landing into the scrub, so had the last down, Stops 5 and 6, dropped along the northeastern leg. All along the five-kilometre cordon paratroopers unbuckled and cached their parachutes and formed up in their four-man sticks, with ten metres between men, ready for action. To protect their rear, Sergeant Derrick Taylor and the three men of his stick moved to mine and ambush the road to the southwest to hold up any FPLM reaction force coming to the aid of ZANLA.

Ahead of the thin line of Rhodesian troops, the Alouette K-Cars were hammering the camp complexes with short staccato bursts of cannon fire.[22]

Squadron Leader Griffiths had made up time so that his ten K-Cars had arrived on time at 0750hrs (H+5) to attempt to stem any northward ZANLA flight out of the 'box'. Two K-Cars peeled off to the left to tackle the Recruits' Camp, five kilometres to the north. Two more immediately attacked the headquarters complex. Another two strafed Chitepo College and its neighbours, Chaminuka and Parirenyatwa camps and the detention barracks. Farther north, a K-Car shot up the Old Garage Camp, a large open-sided tin-roofed building surrounded by 29 huts. Old Garage served as a tool store, a fuel dump, a vehicle graveyard and an ammunition store for the Recruits' Camp. Just to the east of the Old Garage, a K-Car hammered National Stores with bursts of 20mm shells. Finally, at 0752hrs, a pair of K-Cars flew to drive to ground the survivors of the burning and twice-bombed Pasindina 2 Camp, 300 metres to the rear of Stop 1. The reaction there, as

---

[15] email Peter Leid to Chris Cocks, 19 August 2010.

[16] Barbara Cole, *The Elite: The Story of The Rhodesian Special Air Service*, Three Knights Publishing, Amanzimtoti, 1984, p. 182.

[17] MacKenzie, p. 84.

[18] McAleese, p. 134.

[19] Cole, p. 182.

[20] Charlie Warren BCR, *Stick Leader, RLI*, Just Done Publications, Durban, 2007, pp. 177–178.

[21] McDonald.

[22] Binda, p. 252.

Corporal Pete Leid.
Photo: RLIRA

Captain Colin Willis.
Source: Craig Fourie

Corporal Charlie Warren.
Photo: Bruce Kidd

Trooper Keith White.
Photo: RLIRA

elsewhere, was a heavy burst of anti-aircraft fire at K-Car K3. The ZANLA gunners remained undaunted.

The arrival of the K-Cars had allowed McDonald's stick leader to radio for one of them to deal with ZANLA fire pinning his men down. He talked a K-Car onto the target and, under cover of its 20mm cannon fire, led his stick to link up with the rest of their stop group.[23]

At 0754, the Rhodesian cordon was confronted by an attempted breakout by hundreds of running cadres.

Two minutes later, the pilots of ten G-Cars bringing in the 40-man 2 Commando Stop A, pulled up from their treetop flight level, climbed to orientate themselves and then landed to disgorge their troops along a grassy strip behind the northwestern 30-foot-high ridge.

The first two G-Cars deposited two four-man sticks, led by Lieutenant Graeme Murdoch, the officer commanding 8 Troop, on the far right. Murdoch and his men were immediately embroiled in a 40-minute fight to close the ZANLA escape route around the southern end of the ridge.[24] The rest of 2 Commando spilled out into all-round defence for a moment to cover the rapid departure of their helicopters to the admin area. They then sprinted up to the crest of the ridge to engage the ZANLA fugitives in the dense bush of the forward slope.

Sergeant Derrick Taylor.
Photo: RLIRA

One of them, of course, was Lieutenant-Colonel Peter Rich, there to assist Major Simon Haaroff with the complicated radio communications and because, as commanding officer of the RLI, not wishing to miss the show. It meant also that he had joined his son, Lieutenant Michael Rich, the commander of 7 Troop 2 Commander, on the ridge. The father and son took cover close to each other. With tongue in cheek, Colonel Rich would later claim that "as an old shottist", he had time to regret that his son, Michael, "tended to snatch the trigger".[25] In fact, Michael Rich was a fine shot. To Michael it was "quite a unique experience to be in the same assault line as your dad. I recall that there were only two heads sticking up above the grass—his to see if I was okay and mine to see if he was okay. He also kept issuing me instructions/requests out the corner of his mouth like 'Get me a Bakelite AK bayonet' as he couldn't be seen, as the CO, to be grabbing souvenirs."[26]

Lieutenant Graeme Murdoch.
Photo: Jon Caffin

Twenty kilometres to the north, having been led in by Flight Lieutenant Richard 'Bill' Sykes in one of the ten 'Polo' G-Cars, Group Captain Peter Petter-Bowyer and his team set about disembarking their kit and equipment and setting up the admin area and its defence. They were taken aback, however, by the unsuitable nature of the terrain in which they had landed. Far from the clear, flat area that it appeared to be on the air photograph, it was covered with thick, shoulder-high grass interspersed with thick clumps of bush and trees. There was no time to start clearing a landing zone, because, two minutes early, flown by Jack Malloch and his co-pilot, Squadron Leader George Alexander, the commander of No. 3 Squadron, the DC-7 was lining up for its first of a series of parachute drops of pallets of fuel drums. Some of the pallets fell perilously close to

---

[23] McDonald.

[24] email from Graeme Murdoch, 11 August 2010.

[25] Binda, p. 246.

[26] email from Mike Rich, 25 May 2005.

Flight Lieutenant Bill Sykes
Photo: A Pride of Eagles

20mm cannon from an Alouette K-Car above the admin base.
Photo: A Pride of Eagles

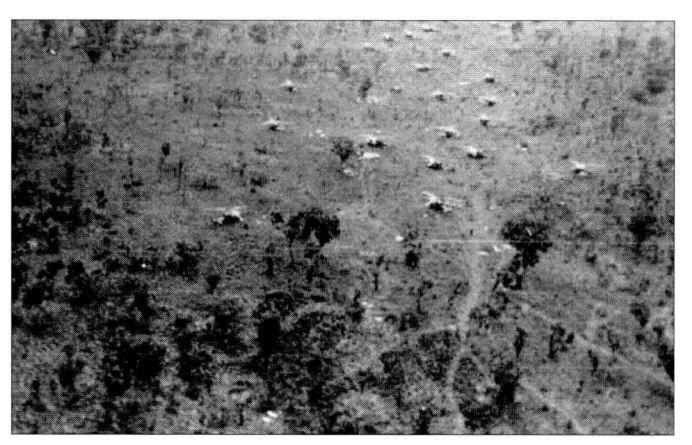

Alouettes parked at the admin base.
Photo: A Pride of Eagles

Petter-Bowyer sets up the admin base communications.
Photo: A Pride of Eagles

the helicopters where men were unloading tools, spares, medical equipment, mortars and crates of ammunition. This raised fears that one or more of the collapsing parachutes might wrap itself around the rotating blades of the idling Polo helicopters. Other pallets fell among the trees.

The drop over, the immediate task of the technicians, Dr Cliff Webster and his medic, the SB men and those of the protection troops who could be spared, was to drop what they were doing to retrieve the scattered drums and roll them through the thick grass where they could be positioned far enough apart for the helicopters that would soon require refuelling. Grass had to be flattened and some trees removed to facilitate aircraft movement and to provide parking for G-Cars waiting to be called back to the battlefield on resupply runs or casualty evacuation and finally the recovery of parachutes and then of men. There was little time to do this before the ten G-Cars flew in after dropping off Haaroff's 2 Commando troopers. K-Cars were due shortly afterward as they ran out of fuel and ammunition.

Captain Ian Buttenshaw, commanding the Support Commando protection troops, had also been surprised by the unsuitable landscape confronting him. He found the area impossible to defend with his 15 men. Nevertheless, he established a mortar position for his two 81mm mortar tubes and their 100 bombs and had a G-Car fly a mortar controller and three men to the hill overlooking the area. The need for manpower to retrieve the scattered fuel drums, however, forced Buttenshaw to leave only one three-man mortar crew manning the tubes and a control post operator to defend the base. Everything depended on the OP spotting anyone approaching the area. Fortunately the location chosen was uninhabited and there was no one to test its defences.

It took two hours before the admin area personnel could concentrate on their own tasks. It was clear, therefore, that any future forward admin area would have to have sufficient men to defend it, to set it up and thereafter to refuel and rearm helicopters, provide first aid and more.[27]

The attack was not yet 15 minutes old but among the shattered buildings and burning huts lay hundreds of dead, wounded or stunned ZANLA personnel. When the Rhodesian troops reached it later, the rows of bodies lying on the parade ground reminded John Cronin of a field of mown corn. Among them were neither Robert Mugabe nor the ZANLA commanders, Josiah Tongogara and Rex Nhongo, something which Walls regretted when speaking to the press later. The wife of Edgar Tekere, Mugabe's mentor (and later his opponent), survived hidden in a latrine.[28]

Yet such was the sustained fire from the anti-aircraft gun pits that every aircraft flying low over the complex after the initial airstrike was hit.[29] Heavy anti-aircraft fire from the Old Garage and the 88 thatched huts of the Ngangas' (herbalists or spiritual healers) Camp prompted Walsh to order a restrike. Red 2 obliged by hammering, with 30mm shells, the Old Garage, its neighbouring National Stores and adjoining huts. In all, the three Hunters of Red Section had fired one thousand rounds. Blue 2 fired 45 Matra 68mm rockets at the mill at Old Stores and added a burst of 140 rounds of 30mm shells into the Ngangas' Camp.

At 0800hrs (H+15) a large group of ZANLA cadres was spotted from the air west of Pasindina 2 Camp outside the waiting Rhodesian cordon. Simultaneously, in the middle of the complex, just south of Chitepo College, an anti-aircraft gun opened fire on a K-Car and hit an accompanying Lynx. The Lynx turned

---

[27] email from Brigadier Ian Buttenshaw, 7 November 2010; Petter-Bowyer, pp. 308–310; Binda, p. 244.

[28] Cole, p. 184.

[29] Cole, p. 183.

away, heading back to Grand Reef, leaking fuel. Walsh called for a response. While two K-Cars swung across to rake Pasindina 2, Red 3 neutralized the gun and then fired rockets and his cannons at a hard core of ZANLA making a stand 200 metres south of the Chaminuka and Parirenyatwa camps and the headquarters.

Walsh flew the command G-Car over the waiting sweeplines, allowing Brian Robinson to identify precisely where all his men were. At 0810hrs, he ordered them to advance. Using co-ordinated fire and movement, the troops moved forward. Orchestrating some 37 callsigns taught Robinson that in future he should wear gloves because his frequent need to press the transmitting pressel switch on his radio handset soon blistered his thumb.

At 0811hrs the first pair of K-Cars, Griffiths' K1 and K1 Alpha left to refuel and rearm at the admin area.

Heavy firing from the Recruits' Camp prompted K4 to call for a Vampire strike. The gunners must have sensed this because their fire slackened off.

Advancing, the 40 men of Stop A pushed their way through the bushy undergrowth on the forward slope of their ridge. As they emerged from its edge, they were confronted by a charge of crouching ZANLA cadres, firing wildly. Controlled rifle and MAG fire broke the charge. Jimmy Swan counted 22 bodies to his front and among them some light-skinned bodies which he assumed were Cubans. The weapons of the fallen were collected, piled up and booby-trapped.

Supported by fire from a K-Car, Stop A skirmished forward to the next tree line only to draw fire, including stick grenades. Again disciplined return fire doused it. Swan counted a further 17 bodies. Supporting fire, including mortars, from Takawira Camp, drove Stop A to ground. They fired back and called for an airstrike.

The 3 Commando Stops 1 and 2 had also run into immediate fire as they moved forward through the bush. Their fierce response drove the ZANLA men back and shortly they were shooting at running figures and firing into likely cover.

Little quarter was being given. The SB wanted to glean information from prisoners but, with no one to spare to guard them, the sweepline left the gathering of them to the mopping-up phase. During Stop 4's advance, MacKenzie caught a ZANLA cadre and had him indicate the ZANLA strongpoints ahead. He handcuffed the prisoner to a bush for later collection and was infuriated when the RLI shot the man on sight.

Although the SAS Stops 4 and 3 of MacKenzie and Willis on his left had brush-filled gullies to their front, they cleared them quickly. They had advanced rapidly by 0826hrs to within 150 metres of the first trench line protecting the Chitepo College and its neighbouring camps, Chaminuka, Parirenyatwa and Nehanda, when Robinson ordered a halt. His reason was that a 12.7mm bullet had holed the main rotor of his G-Car and Walsh was having to fly it gingerly away.

Walsh banked the G-Car away to the north, heading for the admin area to pick up a replacement aircraft. He ordered one of the circling helicopters to pick up Robinson's deputy, Major Mick Graham, to take over for the moment. As Graham was unable

Corporal Jimmy Swan.
Source: Jimmy Swan

Major Mick Graham.
Source: Craig Fourie

to extricate himself from the fighting in the trees and retreat to a safe landing zone, Robinson was forced to stop the advance on the ground and order all the stops to hold their positions until he returned. Walsh handed over control of the air effort to Lynx Alpha 4, flying a close-in reconnaissance orbit. Alpha 4 was promptly also hit but was able to continue its orbit.

As he nursed his Alouette northward, Walsh gave General Walls in the command Dakota an assessment on *Dingo*'s first half an hour. He reported that the New Garage complex was alight. Two-thirds of the tents of Nehanda Camp had collapsed but its anti-aircraft guns were subjecting the K-Cars to heavy fire. Chaminuka Camp appeared untouched and its anti-aircraft guns were still in action. The main building of the headquarters and its accommodation were damaged and there were numerous fires north of the road with the huts in the Matopos and Takawira camps on fire. Huts were alight in Chitepo College but its anti-aircraft guns were still in action.

The National Stores was burning but, despite a large explosion, heavy anti-aircraft fire persisted from there. Farther north the Recruits' Camp was burning and half its huts had been destroyed. To the southwest, Pasindina 2, although half alight, was still the source of anti-aircraft fire.

The bullet strike on Walsh's helicopter had taught a lesson. In any case Walsh would have had to fly to the admin area to refuel shortly, leaving Graham on the ground in charge. After *Dingo*, on future external operations, Walsh and Robinson would fly in the command Dakota, sitting facing each other for ease of discussion and using its superior communications equipment to conduct the operation through their second-in-commands in a Lynx flying over the battle. Another factor in the decision was that the Dakota and Lynx also had incomparable endurance when compared with the helicopter.

0830–0930hrs

After Walsh's arrival, the technicians set to work to transfer his radios to another G-Car. Other helicopters would arrive requiring repairs. A K-Car had also been hit in its rotors. Later the technicians patched one of its main blades and replaced its tail rotors by robbing one of the standby Alouettes. The K-Car flew off to rejoin the battle. The next day Master Sergeant Geoff Dartnell, its technician-air gunner, found that the bullet had lodged in its self-sealing fuel tank. A third helicopter was hit in the engine so a G-Car flew back to Grand Reef to collect a new engine, main blades for Walsh's helicopter and a tail rotor. By the end of the day all aircraft were fit to fly.[30]

Apart from the repairs to be made, there were helicopters to refuel. At 0830hrs, K-Car K6 flew to refuel and rearm. At 0836hrs, replenished K2A returned to the target.

On the battlefield the three stalled sweeplines waited and exchanged fire with ZANLA. Under intensive fire from a heavy machine gun, firing from Chaminuka Camp, Captain Willis of Stop 3 threw smoke to indicate his position and called for an airstrike. K2 responded and called in the Vampires T11s of Voodoo Section.

Before the T11s arrived, a pair of Vampire FB9s of Venom Section strafed the Recruits' Camp again. The Rolls-Royce Goblin engine of Venom 2, however, was severely damaged by either a ricochet or fire from the ground. Squadron Leader Steve Kesby in Venom 1 escorted Venom 2 as its pilot, Philip Haigh (ex-Royal Air Force) attempted to reach Rhodesia. Kesby radioed New Sarum to prepare for an emergency landing but then lost sight of Venom 2 in the cloud. Instead of bailing out, once he crossed the Rhodesian border, Haigh chose to stay with his now-gliding aircraft, its engine seized. One reason could have been that the FB9 lacked an ejection seat so Haigh would have had to turn it upside down and fall out, hoping he was not hit by the tail plane. He achieved a perfect wheels-up landing onto a field in the Inyanga (now Nyanga) district and could have survived if Venom 2 had not hit a ditch and disintegrated, killing him. Few Vampire belly landings were successful because the aircraft was built partly of wood, a legacy of De Havilland's manufacture of the legendary 'wooden wonder', the Mosquito.

At 0844hrs, Voodoo Section silenced the heavy machine gun which had been firing at Willis but, when they came in for a restrike, they drew heavy fire from a multi-barrelled gun sited at the edge of a maize field. Major Haaroff then called for an airstrike on Takawira Camp to the front of Stop A. One of the T11s responded by firing his 60lb rockets. The rockets were old and could be wayward. Seeing a Vampire aiming their way, the 2 Commando stick commanders frantically called on their radios for the pilot to pull out while their men hugged the earth as he fired his rockets and two of them dropped short. Having made his call, Lieutenant Graeme Murdoch dived with his two men on top of their protesting MAG gunner who had taken cover behind the only sizeable tree. Fortunately, the exploding rockets hurt no one.[31]

Simultaneously at 0845hrs, answering a K-Car's instructions, a Hunter attacked Chitepo from south to north, flying over Willis and MacKenzie, with 27 Matra 68mm rockets and 405 30mm shells.

The stalled sweeplines, watching the airstrikes and the ZANLA gun crews firing back, were aware that the bulk of the survivors of New Farm were escaping northward despite the efforts of the K-Cars. The constant need to refuel and rearm meant that there were never enough K-Cars on station to stem the tide. The thin, strung-out line of Rhodesian troops worried also that they would not be able to defeat a determined ZANLA counter-attack. MacKenzie thought a concerted attack by 30 men could break through the Rhodesian cordon but clearly their enemy had not realized just how few troops were confronting them.[32] The exchange of fire continued along the line. Stop 2 was still drawing fire from the riverline.

At 0847hrs the RLI Stop 2 asked K-Car K2A to suppress fire from Chitepo College and Nehanda Camp. This was followed at 0852hrs by a Hunter attack on the multi-barrelled gun there. K-Car K2A continued to attract fire from Chitepo College's neighbouring camps, Parirenyatwa, Chaminuka and Nehanda. Consequently, Willis was asked at 0851hrs to pinpoint the particularly active weapon in Chaminuka Camp for an attack by Hunter Red 3. Then a large-calibre gun at Chitepo College opened up again. Red 3 responded at 0909hrs with a rocket attack on the college and then strafed Stop 2's opponents. Although the

---

[30] Salt, pp. 596–597.

[31] email from Graeme Murdoch, 11 August 2010, Cowderoy & Nesbit, War in the Air, p. 80.

[32] MacKenzie, p. 45.

A G-Car on standby, awaiting further instructions.
Photo: A Pride of Eagles

G-Cars refuelling at the admin area.
Photo: A Pride of Eagles

thickening smoke trapped under the lowering clouds was making air operations dangerous given the number of aircraft orbiting the target areas, at 0919hrs, flying east to west, Red 3 struck all four targets with 68mm rockets and 30mm shells and silenced the Chitepo gun.

Fighting went on with K-Car K6 under rifle fire from National Stores just as his 20mm cannon jammed. He withdrew to clear it.

0930–1100hrs

At 0930hrs, flying the re-equipped spare G-Car, Walsh and Robinson resumed command, albeit from a higher altitude. Immediately, arriving back from New Sarum, White 1 silenced gun pit 1, while Robinson ordered the resumption of the ground attack. Stop 6 on the extreme right flank encountered resistance between National Stores and New Farm's most eastern Thin Camp (twelve huts normally housing 150 ZANLA recruits and six FPLM troops).

On the right flank, Haaroff's Stop A halted on the edge of a tree line just as there was a ZANLA mass charge. Bursts of fire from his 40 men repulsed the charge, leaving 33 cadres dead in the thickets and broken ground. Again the captured weapons were piled up and booby-trapped. Then Stop A resumed their advance, firing into likely cover.[33]

The air attacks continued. At 0933hrs two Vampire T11s of Voodoo Section dived in to strafe the northern half of the Recruits' Camp and an active multi-barrelled gun on the disused rifle range. At 0945hrs Walsh ordered a K-Car to provide covering fire for Cronin's Stop 2 which was still being shot at.

General Walls in the command Dakota, reporting to Combined Operations, claimed the heavy anti-aircraft machine guns had been silenced. Because all the K-Cars had been hit, an attack by the orbiting Canberra was deemed necessary to silence the still-active small-arms fire from Chitepo College and the camp complex of Parirenyatwa, Chaminuka and Nehanda before troops swept them. Fire was also emanating from National Stores and Thin Camp but that would have to be dealt with separately. The cab-ranking Vampire FB9s led the way with a 20mm strafing run through Chitepo College and its neighbours. Close behind them, Canberra Green 3 doused the camps with 300 Mk II Alpha bombs. The bombs were on target but Green 3 was hit twice. Encouraged, Walls ordered a further Canberra Alpha-bomb strike on the ZANLA headquarters and Parirenyatwa Camp.

To weaken the resistance in front of them, Robinson ordered Stops 1–3 to throw smoke to mark targets for a strike by White Section's pair of Hunters parallel to the front line of troops. At 0955hrs White 2 attacked a heavy machine gun firing at him from gun pit 1. Then he and White 1 fired Matra rockets and their 30mm cannons at Matopos and Takawira camps, setting many buildings ablaze. Again the price paid was a bullet hole in a Hunter starboard gun pack. White Section climbed, wheeled and came in again at 1005hrs, firing to assist the resumption of the advance of Stops 1–3, covered by a succession of K-Cars. To the left, Stop A was also moving again.

The aircraft were still attracting fire over two hours after H-Hour. At 1009hrs an orbiting K-Car was fired on from the east of the complex. There also remained the danger of outside interference. At 1020hrs 8 Squadron of the Rhodesian Signals Corps, listening to FPLM broadcasts, heard a message that an anti-aircraft unit had been sent to reinforce ZANLA at New Farm and that infantry units were to follow from Vila de Manica and Catandica. Lynx E4, flying over the nearby roads and railways, reported at 1022hrs that there was no sign of any movement or threat. Then at 1032hrs, he reported that two Land Rovers were approaching. Nothing more was seen of them.

In preparation for the next Canberra strike, Walsh ordered the Vampire FB9s of Venom Section to soften up Chitepo College and Parirenyatwa Camp. Then at 1040hrs Robinson ordered Stops 1–3 to halt their advance to allow the Hunters, Blue 1 and 2, to mark Chitepo College and Parirenyatwa for the incoming Canberra. Blue Section then strafed a ZANLA position 400 metres south of the college and followed that with an attack on Nehanda and Chaminuka camps. Return fire hit Blue 1's starboard windscreen. The troops radioed that every time an aircraft came within range it was fired at.

The thick smoke and dust meant that the Canberra did not see the target marker and dropped its bombs 200 metres north of the target. The Canberra departed to be replaced by another one at 1145hrs.

The depressing news of the moment was confirmation that Haigh had crashed.

1100–1212hrs

In the wake of the Canberra's departure, Robinson ordered Stops 1–3 to continue their advance. As they did, Stop 2 in particular again drew heavy fire as they approached the camp area. This, and the persistent anti-aircraft fire, prompted Robinson at 1110hrs to ask General Walls for permission to withdraw the sweepline if it became bogged down. Walls replied that the advance should continue but it had to avoid getting bogged down.

In response, Robinson ordered the eastern flank to turn northward. At that moment, 1115hrs, the incoming Hunters, Red 1 and Red 2, replacing Blue Section, attacked from the east firing 24 Matra rockets and 520 30mm shells at targets ahead of the troops. Red 1 did not get away unscathed, with a bullet hitting his rear fuselage.

At 1132hrs, called down by K-Car K3 in response to a request by Willis, Red Section suppressed enduring fire from Chitepo College. Under cover of the Hunter attack, Willis's Stop 3 flanked a recoilless rifle and killed the eight-man crew.

At 1156hrs, Robinson ordered the sweepline to close inward.

Stops 3 and 4, Willis and MacKenzie, had come through the trees to face a long zigzag trench line 100 metres in front of them.

---

[33] Binda, p. 256.

Napalm strike.
Photo: A Pride of Eagles

Troop-carrying G-Cars.
Photo: RLIRA

Covered by bursts from their machine-gunners, the SAS troopers charged and seized several hundred metres of trenches only to find a few ZANLA cowering in them. MacKenzie took the opportunity of being in cover to reorganize his men and to have them replenish their magazines and machine-gun belts.

What MacKenzie did not know was that ahead of him on his left, the RLI Stops 1 and 2 had been in the line of some of his fire. John Cronin and his 13 Troop, the nearest half of Stop 2, had to spend ten minutes sheltering behind a brick wall built by Oom Japie Pienaar.[34] 12 Troop of Lieutenant Mark Adams was not so lucky because an SAS bullet wounded his flank man, John Connelly (ex-British Territorial Army, the only casualty suffered in the bush war by Tony Coom's stick while he commanded it). A radioed protest diverted the firing.

In a minute or two, 12 Troop was again under fire, this time from a dug-in 12.7mm DShK Soviet heavy machine gun. Summoned for support by Stop 2, K-Car K4, however, fired at moving figures through the trees' foliage, hitting the Stop 1 stick of Colour Sergeant John Norman (commander of 11 Troop). Shrapnel peppered Norman, Neil Hooley, Paul Furstenburg and M. Grobbler. John Norman was hit in the face. While Peter Leid, the 3 Commando medic, and Furstenburg, the stick medic, were attending to Norman, they were pinned down by an accurate machine-gun burst from a neighbouring stick. It hit Terry Hammond, nearly severing his arm.[35]

Walsh ordered a casevac by G-Car of the wounded. To cover this, at 1200hrs, a Hunter attempted to suppress the ZANLA fire in front of the troops. Adams's Stop 1 then silenced the 12.7mm machine gun and, at 1207hrs, Charles Goatley, flying a G-Car, attempted to fetch the wounded. He drew ZANLA fire and was waved off. Everything had to wait for Stop 1 to clear the area before Coom could talk Goatley in to remove the wounded to the care of Dr Webster at the admin area. Peter Leid travelled with them to tend to Hammond who was bleeding heavily. Hammond survived but was left with a bent, withered arm.[36]

Such was the level of the involvement of the K-Cars, in particular, that at 1212hrs Petter-Bowyer radioed Grand Reef to ask for more 20mm ammunition.

1219–1230hrs

By 1219hrs the sweeplines were close to the camps. Robinson ordered MacKenzie and his Stop 4 to take the Matopos, Takawira and Pasindina 1 camps, beyond the headquarters. Leaving two sticks in a defensive position near the ZANLA headquarters, MacKenzie and 15 SAS men advanced in extended line through the trees toward what he called the 'Intelligence Centre' (presumably the 'registry' at Matopos Camp). En route, he spotted in a clearing a ZANLA four-man gun crew, firing their DShK 12.7mm machine gun from the top of a 30-foot tower. After creeping forward unnoticed, the SAS shot the gun crew and their protection party at the base of the tower. Next, MacKenzie's sweepline encountered another anti-aircraft position, armed

---

[34] Memorandum 'Follow-up to Operation Dingo', Major John R. Cronin, 21 April 1998

[35] Chris Cocks, *Fireforce: One Man's War in The Rhodesian Light Infantry*, Galago, Alberton, 1988, pp. 130-131; email from Peter Leid, 19 August 2010.

[36] Cocks, pp. 130–131; email from Peter Leid, 19 August 2010.

with a twin-barrelled Chinese Type 55 37mm gun (a copy of the Swedish 40mm Bofors). It was unmanned and unused, being still covered with packing grease. Clearly, ZANLA had not yet been trained in its use. If they had been, the Rhodesia Air Force could have suffered serious losses that day. Because it was too heavy to be flown out, MacKenzie would later destroy it with plastic explosive. Moving on through the trees, MacKenzie and his men flushed out and killed some 20 ZANLA cadres hiding behind fallen tree trunks and in holes in a dry riverbed. Some 150 metres farther on, they crossed the trenches defending the Intelligence Centre, a small, empty camp of 18 thatched pole and *dagga* huts serving as offices, classrooms and storerooms. His men searched the huts, finding trunks of documents which MacKenzie and one of his officers browsed through before reserving them for SB inspection later. Among them was a typed ZANLA report on the Selous Scout raid on their Nyadzonya camp that gave the lie to the claims that it had been a refugee camp.[37] McAleese was amazed at just how much was recorded on every ZANLA member.[38] Apart from documents, Corporal Bates Maré discovered a dark room and dozens of modern 35mm Leica, Pentax and Nikon cameras, and two video cameras. The troopers shared them out among themselves. Once MacKenzie had assessed the papers and removed them, the SAS fired the huts and moved back to the rest of Stop 4 near the headquarters.[39]

Also at 1219hrs, Robinson ordered Stop 5 to move through Chitepo College and Parirenyatwa and Chaminuka camps and to halt at the edge of the ploughed fields beyond. Walsh sent K-Car K5 to support Grahame Wilson's Stop 6 as they advanced on the huts around the National Stores.

Simultaneously, Stop 1 overran the dug-in heavy machine gun which had been pinning them down. They found it to be a wheeled DShK 12.7mm gun with plenty of ammunition to hand. They were ordered to mark its position and move on. Over the rest of the ground to the ZANLA headquarters, they encountered only dead bodies.

While Stop 1 was regrouping at the headquarters, they came under inaccurate fire from a ZANLA gunman shooting from a disused brick-making pit in a clump of trees some 200 metres to the northwest. Major Strong ordered Mark Adams and his stick to attack the position. Adams ordered his MAG gunner, Peter Donnelly (an ex-Scots Guardsman), to provide covering fire from a large termite mound to keep the shooter's head down. Then Adams, Bruce Kidd and Digby McLennan executed a left-flanking attack. Donnelly joined them as they charged into the bushes and jumped into the pit only to find it littered with bodies, perhaps the victims of the airstrikes. Among them was their mortally wounded sniper.

Keeping their formation, the stick advanced toward the far edge of the pit. Only Adams had an easy climb out of it and he opened fire to clear the bushes ahead of him and to cover his men still clambering up. What he did not know was that Stop A was advancing beyond the bushes, whose fierce accurate riposte hit Donnelly in the arm, knocking him back into the clay pit. Kidd and McLennan slid down out of sight. Adams hit the ground and crawled backward into the pit, firing his rifle, calling in vain for covering fire. His men did not respond. He dropped into cover, a K-Car flew over and the pilot, Malcolm 'Baldy' Baldwin, radioed, ordering him to throw a red smoke grenade. Adams obliged and the firing stopped.

Stop A had been advancing tactically toward the ZANLA headquarters. The leading extended line had the sticks of Lieutenant Vernon Prinsloo on the left and those of Lieutenant Graeme Murdoch on the right. The command element of Major Haaroff and Lieutenant-Colonel Rich were behind them, followed

---

[37] Reid-Daly, pp. 283–285.
[38] McAleese, p. 136.
[39] MacKenzie, p. 46.

This Lynx, accompanying a K-Car, was hit when an anti-aircraft gun opened up and had to turn back to Grand Reef.
Source: *A Pride of Eagles*

also in extended line by the sticks of Lieutenants Michael Rich and Bob Halkett. Caught in the open by Adams's fire from their left, the front line responded and, led by Prinsloo and Murdoch, skirmished forward using fire and movement. Fortunately, Baldwin flew overhead relaying a message from Major Strong that they were attacking his men. Adams's red smoke grenade confirmed this. Adams returned to the headquarters and called for a casevac. Then Strong ordered Stop 1 to resweep the area and to retrieve the DShK 12.7mm gun.

1230–1400hrs

By 1230hrs the troops had the grim task of clearing and searching the camps. MacKenzie was shown an open-air classroom under the trees which had been devastated by Alpha bombs from a Canberra. Among the blown-over blackboards, 60 ZANLA students lay dead, their bloodied notebooks, filled with quotes from Chairman Mao, strewn around them.

Stops A and 1–3 combed through Pasindina 1, Matopos and Takawira camps, and the headquarters complex. Tony Coom's MAG gunner, John Connelly, clearing a brick ablution building, encountered a locked door and fired through it. His bursts tore into an unseen press of women and children who had taken refuge behind it. (This haunted him for the rest of his life.) Stop 2 advanced on the pig pens in front of the main complex, moving past dead bodies scattered across the ground. The men skirmished forward and began clearing the buildings with grenades. A storeroom yielded nine insurgents who were foolish enough to make a break for it while being interrogated by a stick leader. They were quickly shot dead.

In the shattered and burning headquarters, the troops found documents which were reserved for inspection by the SB members later when it was safe enough to fly them from the admin area. MacKenzie found a bulging briefcase but, before he could examine it, he was ordered by Robinson to take two sticks to the ZANLA motor repair facility at the Old Garage, a kilometre away across the open ground of the centre of New Farm.

In a barn next door to the headquarters, the troops found a quartermaster's store packed with exotic foodstuffs such as tins of Swedish sardines and Israeli orange juice which they consumed despite the SB's prior warnings that they might be poisoned. Later in the afternoon, a SB member stopped one of Cronin's men from taking looted aspirin for a headache, warning they too might be poisoned. Thereafter captured stock was left alone.[40] The store was also filled with sacks of maize meal, sugar, rice and cashew nuts as well as military kit including Soviet and other uniforms.

At Takawira, Stop A had the unpleasant and dangerous task of clearing bunkers with 1kg bunker bombs, killing their occupants. As they searched the camp, the troops spotted ZANLA cadres on the western ridge. They ignored them until two RPG-7 rockets were fired at them. Stop A's riposte killed 14 insurgents, bringing their tally that day to 167 confirmed kills. They moved off to clear the Matopos Camp.[41] The SAS Stops 4, 5 and 6 searched Parirenyatwa, Chaminuka, Nehanda camps and the National Stores and also uncovered food stocks. A member of Stop 4, Andy Johnson, was foolish enough to drink from a can of contaminated condensed milk and had to be flown out by a G-Car for treatment. He recovered but McAleese concluded that he was the victim of the SB's poisoning of clothing and food left in strategic places where ZANLA insurgents might appropriate them.

This activity was not without danger. At 1232hrs, Willis called for an immediate casevac of a serious casualty. Lieutenant Roberts, commander of Stop 5, did likewise at 1254hrs. By then the sweep of camp complexes had killed 50 ZANLA cadres.

The need for airstrikes remained. At 1238hrs, Walsh ordered the two Vampire T11s of Voodoo Section to attack an area near New Farm dams. Ten minutes later the T11s were called to strafe in the vicinity of New Garage. At 1251hrs White Section's Hunters were ordered to strike Pasindina where resistance was impeding Haaroff's Stop A. Four minutes later, talked in by a K-Car, White Section fired 500 30mm cannon shells at a ZANLA group gathering at the river junction northeast of the Recruits' Camp. White Section responded immediately to a call at 1307hrs from Stop A to attack an area between Pasindina 1 and Matopos camps. At 1315hrs an airstrike was demanded to stem a breakout from the National Stores complex. At 1335hrs White Section attacked ZANLA groups at the river junction again before departing and being replaced by the incoming Blue Section. The next in action was Voodoo Section rocketing and strafing a pocket of resistance at Pasindina 1 and coming in again to restrike it.

ZANLA's return fire remained dangerous. At 1314hrs a bullet holed the floor of a K-Car, grazed the forehead and shattered the helmet of Flight Lieutenant Mark McLean, a reservist. G-Car Pink 5 collected a stretcher case from Willis's Stop 3 at 1330hrs and then a 'sitting casualty' from Stop 1. The patrolling Lynx could find no sign of a Mozambican reaction.

At 1350hrs, Robinson deemed it time to fly in the SB members from the admin area to assess and recover the documents and other intelligence material. He took the care to have a K-Car escort their G-Car. After delivering the SB members, both aircraft received an urgent casevac call from Ken Roberts' Stop 5 to uplift a mortally wounded SAS trooper, Frans Nel, and two others. Nel had been shot between the eyes by a ZANLA woman cadre, firing from the New Garage complex. As a precaution, Nel's stick commander, Corporal Trevor Kershaw, ordered his men to turn their caps inside out to hide the 'day-glo' patches which were betraying their presence. The fighting around New Garage, however, made it unsafe for a G-Car to land. It was only at 1512 that a casevac was possible and by then Nel had died. He and Philip Haigh, the Vampire pilot, were the only Rhodesians to die that day. Escorted by a K-Car, Nel's body was flown back to the admin area along with the two wounded men who were stabilized there for their onward journey to hospital in Rhodesia.

---

[40] Cronin.

[41] Cocks, p. 145.

Alouettes waiting their turn to refuel.
Photo: A Pride of Eagles

Drums of avgas lie stacked near a Dakota and a hurrying MAG gunner.
Photo: Claude Botha

1400–1730hrs

Sporadic resistance was still being encountered. This was not surprising considering that 184 men were attempting to search an area of 25 square kilometres. It led Robinson to suggest to General Walls that the mopping up continue until 1600hrs. The G-Cars would then fly the troops and their equipment back to the admin area. The men would spend the night there and then be flown back to Rhodesia the next day. Walls agreed to reassess the position at 1530hrs.

At 1400hrs, to deal with firing from the bush west of Pasindina 1, Robinson ordered Haaroff's Stop A to "pull back and a Hunter strike will be put in. You are then to have another go".

Fifteen minutes later, Stop A marked the target with white phosphorus and Blue 1 and 2 raked it with six 68mm rockets and 600 30mm shells.

The thickening weather forced Walsh to cancel the Vampire cab-rank which left White Section's Hunters to provide air support until their low fuel state forced them to leave at 1545hrs.

Adhering to the original plan, which meant the troops would be withdrawn before dusk, two Canberras were loaded at New Sarum with eight delayed-fused 500lb bombs and four with instantaneous fuses. The delayed bombs were meant to surprise, harass or kill any ZANLA personnel returning to the camp during the night.

By 1500hrs most of the main camps had been cleared. Weapons, ammunition, kit, equipment and documents had been collected, assessed and sorted for recovery or demolition. Robinson ordered the flying in of demolition kits for this purpose. Because of the lack of heavy lifting helicopters and the withdrawal tasks already facing the Alouettes, most of the prized new anti-aircraft guns had to be spiked. Acknowledging the work still to be done, General Walls agreed at 1520hrs to the troops continuing their mop-up until 1600hrs, provided they could be withdrawn to the admin area by last light. He added a warning that the cloudy weather was making it difficult for helicopters to land at Lake Alexander. The deadline, however, could not be met. No one had yet been to the Recruits' Camp. By 1545hrs, Grahame Wilson's Stop 6 still lacked demolition kits and at 1555hrs the SB team was told to move to Chaminuka Camp where a formidable collection of documents had been discovered. Robinson ordered additional SB members to be flown in from the admin area.

Another arriving from there was Group Captain Petter-Bowyer, asked by Walls to assess the effect of his new weapons. Petter-Bowyer was shaken by the carnage.[42]

The G-Cars removed equipment and other items and then at 1720hrs began a shuttle, conveying Haaroff's troops back to the admin area for the night.

With only an hour of light left, Robinson realized that a total withdrawal before nightfall was impossible. He warned Stops 1–6 that they would have to stay the night at New Farm and be ready by first light, at 0545hrs of 24 November, for withdrawal via the admin area to Lake Alexander and Grand Reef.

To deter any ZANLA/FPLM interference with it, the withdrawal would be preceded by airstrikes. The air force deferred its bombing of New Farm that night to the next.

Robinson ordered Stops 1–3 to recover the parachutes from the morning's drop zone and then camp for the night near the ZANLA headquarters. Stop 4 was to remain at Chaminuka Camp and Stops 5 and 6 to stay where they were at New Garage.

In his final report of the day, Robinson estimated that 500 ZANLA cadres had been killed and 20 captured at the cost of two Rhodesians killed and twelve wounded, seven of them by 'friendly fire'.

---

[42] Petter-Bowyer, p. 312.

1730–0530hrs

Stops 1–3 recovered as many of their parachutes as they could but some, like Mike McDonald's snagged parachute and his jump helmet, had been burned in one of the many bush fires started by the action.[43] The men loaded them onto the G-Cars, shuttling back and forth from the admin area, and then moved into a defensive position for the night southwest of the ZANLA headquarters.

MacKenzie's Stop 4 set up all-round defence with his headquarters in a bomb crater in an entrenched area in the trees at Chaminuka Camp. Stops 5 and 6 did likewise at New Garage.

As dusk fell on the smouldering camps, an SAS corporal raised the green and white national flag of Rhodesia on a tree, signifying the expropriation of territory, at least for the night.

At the admin base, the helicopter shuttle to Lake Alexander removed as much equipment and men as could be done before dark. The trip, however, was not without drama. Flying over hostile territory, the G-Car carrying Jimmy Swan's stick was hit by two bullets. The pilot made a forced landing on an island in the Chicamba Real Dam, close to the mountainous Rhodesian border. The crew and the four 2 Commando men, low on ammunition, had a nervous wait in the fading light until a helicopter arrived with spares. Once repaired, the helicopter flew to Lake Alexander to refuel before flying to New Sarum to be inspected in preparation for Zulu 2, the attack on Tembué.

It had been a long, exhausting day. The helicopter commander, Squadron Leader Harold Griffiths, for example, had flown for nine hours and thirty-five minutes.[44] At the admin area those of Haaroff's 2 Commando troops left behind had the comfort of piles of parachutes to sleep on. In addition, they were rewarded with a tot of Bols brandy in their coffee poured by Lieutenant-Colonel Peter Rich from his water bottle.

Captain Cliff Webster took the moment to remonstrate with Rich for having hazarded a double tragedy by sharing the battlefield with his son and for not dropping prone when under fire. His weary commanding officer patted him on the shoulder and explained, "Dakari, I am getting old and I was so f....d running through the bush I knew that if I lay down I would never get up again."[45]

By contrast, the night at New Farm was anything but comfortable. After dark, ZANLA stragglers returned, thinking the departing helicopters had removed all the troops. To identify themselves, they called out "Comrade, Comrade." The Rhodesian troopers replied, "Comrade" and then fired on them as they approached.[46] In total, some 60 cadres were killed that night in the skirmishes.

---

[43] McDonald.

[44] Flying log of H.G. Griffiths, Vol. 4.

[45] emails from Dr Cliff Webster, 3 September 2009 and Graeme Murdoch, 11 August 2010.

[46] McAleese, p. 137.

0530–1900hrs

At 0530hrs the clearance patrols around the Rhodesian positions were given air cover by the arrival of a pair of Hunters, one armed with frantan and the other with Matra rockets. They were accompanied by two photo-reconnaissance Canberras.

In their wake came Walsh and Robinson in their G-Car, K-Cars, Red Section's three Hunters and a Canberra loaded with Alpha bombs.

The aircraft began attacking suspected ZANLA positions. At 0545hrs Red Section dropped four frantan bombs on a suspected ZANLA hideout and then was called in to attack Nehanda Camp. Simultaneously, the Canberra disgorged its bouncing Alpha bombs along the densely bushed riverline, prompting a burst of return fire.

The Hunters established the cab-rank for the day and would rotate it with the Vampires. The cab-rank was intended to last for five hours while the men on the ground wrapped up the operation. The Lynxes and K-Cars orbited constantly, looking for signs of any threat to the operation on the ground. All the while Walsh kept a wary eye on the weather.

At 0605hrs General Walls radioed Walsh and Robinson from his command Dakota, back in its orbit north of New Farm. He asked for the plan for the day and was told that the G-Cars would assemble at the admin area to wait for the completion of the clearing, demolition and recovery of parachutes and what ZANLA weapons that could be salvaged.

The troops continued their sweeps through the destroyed camps which still yielded grisly surprises. MacKenzie's men happened on a further 70 dead bodies. Then the old farmhouse of the ZANLA headquarters yielded a further surprise in the form of four bodies with hands bound behind their backs, executed by ZANLA before the attack. They had been shot in the back of their heads.

MacKenzie had gone there to look for the briefcase that he had found on the previous day. He had hoped it might have belonged to the ZANLA paymaster but it turned out to contain documents and a new Rolex watch. The documents would be passed on to the SB team when they arrived but he kept the watch at the suggestion of his men and later sold it for more than a month's pay.[47]

By 0600hrs, the other stop groups had completed their searches but not yet the demolition of weapons, ammunition and stores for which they needed explosives. They moved to the drop zone to pick up the remaining parachutes and jump helmets. Robinson detached Stop 1 to clear Pasindina 2, the westernmost camp, which hitherto had only been attacked from the air and whence small arms were still firing at the aircraft. Stop 1 would find that all bodies but one had been removed from Pasindina 2. They shot one insurgent and captured another. They found documents, maps and, what they did not admit to, two folding-butt FN rifles, much prized by paratroopers. Mark Adams took one and Tony Coom the other.

---

[47] McAleese, p. 137.

G-Cars in flight, observed by an adjacent pilot.
Photo: Warwick Hodgson

82mm mortar and crew.
Photo: The Saints

By 0735hrs, Stops 2, 3, 5 and 6 had recovered all the parachutes they could and signalled for their removal by the G-Cars waiting at the admin area. They returned to the camp complexes to get on with the demolition.

General Walls gave ComOps his first assessment that "at worst, [the] job was worthwhile, at best [it] may have been bloody excellent". He believed the standing tally of 560 kills to be an underestimate because no one yet on the ground had assessed what had happened at Pasindina 2, the Recruits' Camp, and in other areas. He welcomed that there had been no mention on any broadcast of the attack. He closed with the comment that the weather was not helping the top cover or the movement of helicopters.[48]

The war within Rhodesia intruded with 3 Brigade, Umtali, asking for a Lynx to assist with a follow-up on a sighting of 20 insurgents. Walls released the Lynx and helicopters and offered troops from the reserve.

MacKenzie met the SB team at the headquarters to hand over the briefcase and then suggested to Robinson, who agreed, that he and his men should search the Old Garage complex and destroy its fuel dump and vehicles.

As they walked there they could hear the explosions and bursts of fire as the other stops began their demolitions and encountered pockets of ZANLA personnel. Willis and his Stop 3 used explosive charges to destroy a 75mm recoilless rifle, a Mercedes 2.5-tonne ambulance, a Peugeot 504 sedan and two Gestetner roneo machines.

They set fire to medical supplies with phosphorus. They demolished three typewriters with an axe and bent the barrels and broke the stocks of 25 SKS rifles.

At 0900hrs Robinson reported all this to General Walls, adding that he was sending Grahame Wilson and his Stop 6 to clear the Recruits' Camp. He hoped to fly out all the troops by 1200hrs.

At 0905hrs MacKenzie informed Robinson that he and his men had not only found more vehicles at the Old Garage site but also had wiped out 40 ZANLA personnel hiding in a nearby *donga* (ditch) after an initial exchange of fire. Among the dead was Lazarus Mandeya, the commander of the ZANLA transport section. It took MacKenzie's men an hour and 40 minutes to complete their demolition of Old Garage's well-equipped workshop and office, its petrol and diesel tanks, two diesel engines, a bus, a ten-tonne truck, a Commer pick-up truck, five motorcars, including a large new BMW and a Land Rover. They bent the barrels and broke the stocks of 45 various small arms and blew apart the new twin 37mm Chinese anti-aircraft gun.

While this was being done, MacKenzie drove off in a white Peugeot light truck which had been serviced at a service station in Salisbury only three weeks previously before it was stolen and driven over the border. He used it to collect 13 DshK 12.7mm guns from the anti-aircraft positions so that they could be flown out. As he drove, he heard on the command channel two Hunters conclude that his white truck was carrying a group of escaping ZANLA. His transmission of "Stop, stop" drew a response from General Walls in the command Dakota, ordering off the Hunters.[49]

Ken Roberts and his Stop 5 dealt with the stock at New Garage and in the process surprised and killed two cadres. Stop 5 used phosphorus to burn 75 tyres, complete sets of vehicle spares and tools and a small quantity of maize. With demolition charges they destroyed eight barrels of oil, a new generator plant, a new compressed air plant, a new John Deere tractor, an ambulance and a 4.5-tonne truck. They bent the barrels and smashed the butts of 30 SKS rifles.

Flown to the Recruits' Camp at 1055hrs in six G-Cars, escorted by three K-Cars, Wilson found 31 dead bodies and a great many trails of blood. He estimated the camp held 700 people. The time constraint precluded a thorough search and no resistance was

---

[48] BECM RAAP, Box 844, ComOps TAC HQ to ComOps, 24 November 1977.

[49] MacKenzie, p. 46.

encountered so Stop 6 concentrated on burning an estimated 40 tons of clothing, 40 bags of maize and ten tons of medical supplies. They used explosive charges to destroy a grinding mill, 5,500 12.7mm and 14.5mm rounds, seven 12.7mm gun barrels and a complete 82mm mortar. They punctured 10–12 tons of tinned food and bent the barrels and broke the stocks of 200 SKS rifles. The SB team was flown in to assess the documents found and had them flown out by a G-Car.

In the final clearance of main complexes, the troops had found and destroyed a further DShK 12.7mm gun. Finally they set fire to all unburned structures, a task which experience had taught them had its dangers because ammunition was often hidden in the thatch. Two anti-tank landmines were laid in the main access road from Chimoio and anti-personnel mines planted at random in the camps.

By 1200hrs the helicopter shuttle of men, parachutes and equipment had begun with the flying out of Stops 1 and 2 to the admin area from where the Polo G-Cars took them to Lake Alexander where military police awaited to frisk them of all forbidden loot. In the event, there were too few MPs to handle the number of constantly arriving troops as the shuttle went on through the afternoon.

The trip from the admin area was not without incident. The G-Car carrying Tony Coom's stick ran low of fuel and had to find one of the fuel caches which the Rhodesian security forces positioned in the border areas.

Before they left, MacKenzie's men set up the RAMS beacons for the night's bombing by Canberras. Invented by the Rhodesians, the RAMS (radio-activated marker system) comprised two flares set at prescribed distances from a target which were ignited by a radio signal from an approaching Canberra to enable it to bomb accurately at night.[50]

All resistance at New Farm had not been quelled because a Dakota dropping pamphlets was fired at.

By 1740hrs the airlift out of Mozambique was over. The helicopter crews flew from Lake Alexander to Grand Reef where the Dakotas were flying troops in relays to New Sarum to prepare them for Zulu 2, the attack on the ZANLA camp at Tembué. The 48 paratroops of Support Commando were driven back to Salisbury, their commander, Major Nigel Henson, in the staff car of Lieutenant-Colonel Rich. Having spent two hot days, kitted up, waiting in the shade of the wings of their Dakotas for a call to reinforce the effort at Chimoio, the turn of Support Commando to jump on Operation *Dingo* was coming.

Treated to a three-course dinner including strawberries and cream, the helicopter crews spent the night at Grand Reef before flying the next day to Mtoko also in preparation for the next phase.

The final act at New Farm, Chimoio, was the dropping of six delay-fused 500lb bombs that night by a Canberra guided by the RAMS.

The final figure of the ZANLA casualties, dead and wounded, was unknown. The troops had never counted. Some put it in the thousands. At the cost of two dead and twelve wounded, Zulu 1 had achieved its aims. The wealth of intelligence gained, the high kill rate and its harassing value, made Zulu 1 not only the first and most successful of Rhodesian camp attacks but also created the template for future operations.

---

[50] Petter-Bowyer, p. 276.

CHAPTER EIGHT:
IAN SMITH'S DECLARATION, 24 NOVEMBER 1977

Air Vice-Marshal Harold Hawkins.
Photo: A Pride of Eagles

At 1600hrs, as the airlift was underway and, because Zulu 1 had struck the blow he intended and Zulu 2 might double its impact on the standing and the threat posed by ZANU (Mugabe) and ZANLA, Ian Smith made his move.

At Government House in Bulawayo, he declared that, because the latest Anglo-American initiative had failed to achieve a settlement between the Rhodesian Government and all its opponents, including the 'external' nationalists (Mugabe and Nkomo), he would settle with the 'internal' nationalists led by Bishop Muzorewa.

He added that the basis of the new constitution would be full adult suffrage and he promised the existing mainly white electorate the chance to approve it in a referendum before a general election brought in a majority rule government in 1978. In the event, the process took longer and the election was only held in April 1979.

Nkomo responded immediately, declaring that the war would continue and that Smith was merely buying time by gathering his 'stooges' around him. The Mozambican Government ignored Smith's commitment and instead expressed its outrage at the attack on New Farm to Rhodesia's only ally, South Africa.

Consequently, the South African diplomats muttered threateningly to the Rhodesians about withdrawing their helicopters. Previously in 1976 after the furore over the Nyadzonya raid, they had temporarily withdrawn their helicopter pilots serving in Rhodesia. The Rhodesian diplomatic representative in Pretoria, Air Vice-Marshal Harold Hawkins, replied that the strike had been a pre-emptive one on 3,000–4,000 ZANLA cadres fresh from training in Tanzania and poised to enter Rhodesia. He made a parallel to the South African raids into Angola. Nevertheless, the South African Secretary for Foreign Affairs, Brand Fourie, warned that the Rhodesians would again be accused of using military action to wreck a political initiative, this time the Anglo-American proposals.

CHAPTER NINE:
THE PREPARATION FOR THE ATTACK ON TEMBUÉ

Adhering to the plan on Friday, 25 November 1977, the helicopters flew from Grand Reef, Umtali, to the airfield at Mtoko. From there on D-Day, Saturday, 26 November, they would begin their journey to Tembué. They would refuel at the forward airfield at Mount Darwin and fly on to the helicopter assembly area where they would be joined by the repaired helicopters flown in from New Sarum. Refuelled, rearmed and loaded with stores and specialist teams, the next leg of their journey would be to 'The Train' helicopter staging post. The last leg was across Cabora Bassa Dam to the forward administration area eleven kilometres southwest of the ZANLA camp at Tembué.

At New Sarum that day, the SAS and Support Commando paratroops, the 3 Commando paratrooper reserve, the 2 Commando protection troops and the aircrew, showered and dressed in fresh uniforms. They cleaned their weapons and drew new maps and gridded air photos.

The Director of Air Operations then conducted the final air briefing of the officers commanding New Sarum and Thornhill, the squadron commanders, section leaders and K-Car pilots. The Rhodesian Air Force would field seven Hunters, five Vampires, four Canberras, the command Dakota and six Dakotas carrying 144 paratroopers, Jack Malloch's DC-7, four Lynxes, and 31 helicopters, namely the command G-Car, eight K-Cars, twelve G-Cars and ten South African Polo G-Cars.

The main briefing of unit commanders followed at 0900hrs in the SAS model room at Cranborne Barracks. Captain Dubois of the RIC had produced another polystyrene and plaster of Paris model. Captain Scott McCormack, Major Brian Robinson and Group Captain Norman Walsh described the details of the plan of the attack on the three-camp complex and the withdrawal thereafter.

The aim of the operation was the same as that of Zulu 1, namely: to kill or capture the maximum number of ZANLA personnel, the gathering of intelligence and the destruction of the camps, supplies and war matériel.

The briefers discounted the likelihood of any effective FPLM response to the attack. They reiterated that the base was not just the site of the ZANLA headquarters for Tete Province, directing the incursions into northeastern Rhodesia, but also a specialist training centre. This meant it would still have at least the heavy-calibre weapons reported in July 1977. The initial airstrike on D-Day, 26 November 1977, on all three camps would be timed at 0800hrs (H-Hour) because it was understood that was the time when the muster parades were held.

Again the constraints of manpower meant that there would be only enough paratroopers to box in Camps B and C. Camp A was the counterpart of the Recruits' Camp at Chimoio as it housed 1,000 trainees, staff and six FPLM troops in 178 thatched huts. Even though it was thought to contain two heavy machine guns, two KPV 14.5mm anti-aircraft guns, one 82mm mortar and a 75mm recoilless rifle, it would be left to be dealt with by the Vampires and other aircraft while the troops cleared the other

Jack Malloch's DC-7.
Photo: *A Pride of Eagles*

two camps. The weapons held by Camp C were not known but Camp B was believed to have one heavy machine gun, two KPV 14.5mm anti-aircraft guns and two 75mm recoilless rifles. Camp B had an estimated population of 500 trained personnel acquiring advanced specialist skills. Its FPLM detachment was thought to be four to six men. In the 53 huts of Camp C was a similar FPLM detachment living with 150 fully trained ZANLA cadres ready for deployment.

As before, the jet aircraft would use New Sarum for refuelling and rearming. The Dakotas would fly from New Sarum but return to and base themselves at Mount Darwin as its airfield was the nearest to the target which had a 940-metre runway capable of taking them.

The 48-man 3 Commando paratrooper reserve would be based there along with an air force air traffic controller, technical staff and supplies and 150 drums of fuel for the Dakotas and Lynxes.

The helicopter assembly area at the airstrip at Chiswiti, the refuelling stage on 'The Train' and the forward administration area would be similarly equipped with fuel, supplies and air traffic controllers, personnel to serve the needs of the troops in action and protection for helicopters using them.

After the unit commanders had briefed their men, the RLI 'land-tail' convoy transported northward the 48-man 3 Commando para reserve, the 2 and Support Commando protection troops with their mortars for Chiswiti and 'The Train', the air force controllers, army administration and medical staff, SB, quartermaster teams and 240 drums of fuel. At Mount Darwin, the convoy dropped off the 3 Commando troops and went on to set up the helicopter assembly point at Chiswiti.

At 1800hrs the helicopters and Lynxes arrived at Mount Darwin. At the same moment seven Hunters landed at New Sarum from their base at Thornhill, Gwelo.

CHAPTER TEN:
THE ATTACK ON TEMBUÉ, 26–27 NOVEMBER 1977

Zulu 2 began at 0510hrs on Saturday, 26 November 1977, with the lift-off from Mount Darwin of Yellow Section's ten South African Polo G-Cars. They flew to Chiswiti to refuel and then left for 'The Train' in Mozambique, landing there at 0600hrs. Yellow Section disembarked Squadron Leader Rex Taylor and his assistant, an air force armourer, two medics, two members of SB and Major Simon Haaroff and 15 2 Commando men. The team unloaded nine drums of jet fuel, two 60mm mortars, bombs, aircraft ammunition, spares, radios and other equipment. What had not been done in the preceding days was for someone to have examined the suitability of the dropping zone for the fuel drums to be delivered by the DC-7.

Flying out of Mount Darwin were eight K-Cars, their ammunition trays loaded with 440 20mm rounds, and the command G-Car flown by Group Captain Norman Walsh and carrying Major Brian Robinson. They were followed into the air by Pink Section's twelve Rhodesian G-Cars carrying Group Captain Peter Petter-Bowyer and his forward administration-area team and their equipment and supplies. At 0635hrs the K-Cars arrived at 'The Train' to refuel followed shortly by the G-Cars.

At New Sarum, Salisbury, while boarding his Dakota, Major Nigel Henson noticed the pilot was wearing a parachute, something not normally done. The six Dakotas took off at 0625hrs, carrying their 144 SAS and Support Commando paratroopers. Later the formation would fly so low over Lake Cabora Bassa that Henson could see eddies on its surface created by the wash of the propellers.[51]

At 0700hrs the DC-7 left New Sarum, carrying 20 fuel drums for 'The Train' and 40 fuel drums and 2,500 rounds of 20mm K-Car ammunition for the forward admin area, along with Lieutenants Graeme Murdoch and Vernon Prinsloo and their 14 2 Commando protection troops and two 60mm mortars.

At 'The Train' refuelling was completed and at 0705hrs the K-Cars and the command helicopter lifted off, flying northeastward, intending to arrive over Tembué at 0805hrs.

Ten minutes later, at 0715hrs, Pink Section's twelve G-Cars left 'The Train' for the forward admin area hoping to arrive at 0815hrs. Aboard were Peter Petter-Bowyer and his team.

At 0720hrs the Hunters of Red, White and Blue Sections, the Canberras of Green Section and the Vampires of Venom Section were airborne. Below and ahead of them at 0730hrs Walsh reported weather clear. At 0750hrs Venom Section reported they would be two minutes late.

Arriving earlier than expected, Pink Section's G-Cars landed at the forward admin area at 0758hrs. This time Petter-Bowyer found it suitable. His teams unpacked their kit and the spares, ammunition and equipment. At 0815hrs, standing on the roof of his G-Car, he guided the DC-7 by radio to the dropping zone. Again, however, the drop went awry. The pilots, Jack Malloch and Squadron Leader George Alexander, flew below the safe height of 300 feet above ground to drop the paratroopers and their heavy containers. The result was injured men and damaged weapons. Lieutenants Murdoch and Prinsloo were first out of the door. Though Murdoch landed safely, Prinsloo's canopy twisted and he suffered a hard landing with the base plate of a 60mm mortar still strapped to his leg but fortunately in the soft mud of a *vlei* (marsh). The *vlei* also spared Corporal Jimmy Swan and his 60mm mortar any damage. He recalls cutting one trooper out of the tree on which his parachute had snagged, and the medics

---

[51] email from Nigel Henson, 27 May 2009.

Paras waiting to emplane for the second phase of Operation *Dingo*, the strike on Tembué.
Photo: *A Pride of Eagles*

patching up the injured and preparing them for later evacuation.[52] Next, once the paratroops had secured the area, the 40 drums and the ammunition boxes were dropped and scattered over a wide area, 1,800 square metres, and one parachute candled.[53] One or two drums nearly killed a local Mozambican who had been detained earlier and tied to a tree. The team immediately set to work, collecting, rolling and positioning the drums in clumps to facilitate multiple refuelling. Later the technicians would have to change a stricken helicopter engine with one flown in from New Sarum via 'The Train'.

A difficulty experienced was that the army radios proved inadequate and a public address system was needed to give orders across the sprawling refuelling and helicopter parking areas.[54]

0800hrs (H-Hour)

On time at 0800hrs six Hunters dived in to rocket, strafe and bomb the three ZANLA camps at Tembué, while the seventh orbited above ready to supplement their efforts.

Blue Section, Flight Lieutenant Blythe-Wood and Air Lieutenant Lowrie, strafed Camp A with rockets and 800 30mm shells. They reported that 80 per cent of the target was destroyed and that people were seen running to the riverline.

Red 1, Squadron Leader Richard Brand, opened the attack on Camp B with a 30mm cannon barrage followed by Red 2's two 50-gallon frantan bombs which hit the target.

White Section, Flight Lieutenant Spook Geraty and Squadron Leader Vic Wightman, dived down, releasing four canister-loads of flechettes over Camp C and strafing it with 750 cannon shells. The whistling, jostling flight of 18,000 six-inch steel darts struck an empty target, the parade ground at Camp C. The expectation of striking the 0800hrs muster parade had led their inventor, Petter-Bowyer, to press for the use of the flechettes. The muster parade had been held at 0430hrs, after which the ZANLA personnel had broken into small groups as they did every day. In any case, Camp B, not C, was the principal camp. Furthermore, 1,000 trained men had moved to a new camp 15.3 kilometres to the north and 500 to Bene to the south on the previous day. That left 3,500 personnel in Camps A, B and C. Regret would be expressed at the debrief of Zulu 2 that a percussion weapon, such as the 450kg Golf bomb, had not been used. Walsh had ruled out the use of the flechettes at New Farm, Chimoio, because of the inevitable international outcry after the expected inspection by international agencies such as the UN High Commission for Refugees. He did not anticipate such inspections at the remote Tembué camp. Flown in later in the day to inspect the strike, Petter-Bowyer found the parade ground was littered with pink plastic tail fins and steel shafts buried deep into the earth. A lone tree was festooned with the darts from its top to its base.

Covering the approaching Canberras, Red Section silenced the AA guns and set the sleeping quarters alight in Camp B with a salvo of 24 Matra 68mm rockets and 400 30mm cannon rounds.

---

[52] email from Graeme Murdoch, 11 August 2010; Binda, p. 270.

[53] BECM RAAP, Box 844, Op *Dingo*, radio message, 26 November 1977.

[54] Petter-Bowyer, p. 310.

A Dakota flies troops over the Cabora Bassa Dam.
Photo: A Pride of Eagles

G-Cars over Cabora Bassa.
Photo: A Pride of Eagles

Flying at the optimum height and speed for bombing with Mk II Alpha bombs, 300 feet above the ground and 350 knots, the four Canberras released 1,200 of them over Camp B. Their direction, however, was wrong and their bombs missed much of the camp, striking only a dozen of the 70 huts. Many bombs exploded harmlessly in the bush beyond the camp. The shrapnel from the airbursts also had no effect on the thick roofs of the anti-aircraft and mortar positions.

Consequently, the Hunters faced heavy machine-gun fire when they returned to restrike Camp B. What had been needed to attack the gun positions was frantan.

Following the Hunters came three Vampires blasting Camp A with 60lb squash-head rockets and 20mm cannon shells.

0804–0810hrs

As at New Farm, Chimoio, two days previously, most of the inhabitants of the camps, aside from the anti-aircraft gunners, scattered. People were seen fleeing to the cover of the nearby riverbed as, at 0804hrs, Squadron Leader Griffiths, the K-Car leader, ordered the Hunters to break off because his K-Cars were overhead the camps. Blue Section responded by proposing to strafe the riverline west of Camp A where so many of its inmates had run.

A K-Car attack on the tin-roofed garage and its vehicles ignited the fuel stored there. The K-Cars over Camps B and C were immediately under fire from a 12.7mm machine gun firing from the east.

Following a complicated plan of south-to-north and west-to-east flights, the Dakotas droned across the area, spewing long lines of paratroopers, attempting to form a tight box around Camp C. They aimed to place Henson's two Support Commando 24-man stops, Lieutenant Michael Webb's Stop 1 and Lieutenant Neill Jackson's Stop 2, on the north and east sides. Grahame Wilson's SAS Stop 6 was supposed to land to the south and Ken Roberts' Stop 5 across the river to the west. There were insufficient troops to do the same for Camp C so MacKenzie's Stop 4 formed a blocking position across the river while Willis's Stop 3 did likewise in the south leaving the K-Cars to attempt to deter any flight. Of course, no one yet knew that Camp B and not Camp C should have been the main target.

Feeling they were dropped too close to their target, the paratroopers descended among hundreds of fleeing ZANLA cadres. Major Henson recalls seeing many running figures underneath him as he dropped among the mopane trees to land in short grass. His troops formed a stop line and waited, killing some 30 to 40 insurgents who blundered into it.[55]

Although the ZANLA gunners hit some aircraft, no serious damage was inflicted. In addition, the Rhodesians did not suffer a single fatality that day. They came close to suffering one when an SAS sergeant's life was saved by the tree that his tangled unopened canopy snagged, braking his fall. Dropping from 450 feet, he had no time to deploy his reserve parachute.[56]

0810–0917hrs

As Norman Walsh and Brian Robinson took over command of the air and ground forces respectively, the pilots in the orbiting aircraft could see the troops of the FPLM garrison at Tembué village, two kilometres northeast of Camp A, making it plain they would not intervene. They were standing on roofs, watching the action. The Lynxes orbiting outside the target area soon confirmed there was no movement toward it from the village or on the road from Bene to the south. The forward admin area also had no traffic approaching it, perhaps because the nearest road seemed to have been cut.

Around Camps B and C, the Rhodesian troops were getting into their formations to be ready to move. While they did this, at 0810hrs, K-Car K2 asked Blue Section's Hunters to silence a

---

[55] email from Nigel Henson, 27 May 2009.

[56] Cole, p. 188.

Dingo 2 admin base.
Photo: *A Pride of Eagles*

ZANLA position firing at him from near the garage. Robinson responded by ordering the stop groups to throw smoke grenades to indicate their positions as an aid to the strike.

At 0823hrs, because Wilson's Stop 6 had been dropped too far to the west and across the river, Walsh ordered K-Cars K1 and K2 to block any flight to the south from Camp C. Robinson followed with orders to Wilson to cross the river to Stop 6's intended southern blocking position. He added a warning to Wilson that he could see trenches filled with ZANLA insurgents ahead of Stop 6's eastward march. Robinson also had Ken Roberts's Stop 5, blocking Camp C to the west to move into the trees of the riverline to prevent escape down it

As he concentrated on guiding the sweeplines closing on their two camps, Robinson had distractions. Willis asked Robinson for a casevac for an injured man whom he left behind with a man to protect him. Neill Jackson of Stop 2, closing in on Camp C from the east, requested a replacement for a damaged radio. Then at 0847hrs, General Peter Walls from the command Dakota demanded from Robinson an estimate of ZANLA casualties. With the K-Cars warning the troops of entrenchments and pockets of resistance and the need to pick up Stop 3's casualty, Robinson had too many distractions to make any calculation.

He replied tersely, "Not yet."

In the event, his companion moved the casualty westward to the Tembué–Bene road because there was no open space in the bush for a helicopter to land.

At 0855hrs a K-Car pilot, out of ammunition, called for a Hunter attack on a 20-man ZANLA group west of the river. Flight Lieutenant Abram obliged with an initial 120-round burst from his cannons and returned to fire 18 68mm rockets. The next Hunter attack was ordered by Robinson to deal with any resistance ahead of Wilson's advance on Camp C. Robinson wanted Webb's Stop 1 to clear the area of the strike but they were too far from it to oblige him.

The ZANLA response to the converging sweeplines was sufficiently muted to allow G-Car Pink 4 to deliver two replacement radios to Stop 1 and to collect Stop 3's casualty.

At 0917hrs ComOps relayed a progress report from Walls to the headquarters of the army and the air force. Walls stated it was, "Too early to assess numbers but prospects good for [a] bad day for floppies [insurgents]. Some heavy guns but appears those remaining now not manned. K-Cars have slain at least a few score by the sound of it but this unconfirmed. Appears only one jump casualties [sic]. Construction group to NE took gap, no sign of [FPLM] interference at this stage."[57]

0924–1015hrs

At 0924hrs, departing the target to refuel at the forward admin area, Walsh and Robinson issued their last orders before SAS Major Mick Graham, being flown in one of the Lynxes, deputized for Robinson. Robinson ordered MacKenzie's Stop 4 and Roberts's Stop 5 to cover the riverline to intercept anyone running between Camps B and C. Walsh demanded more refuelled and rearmed K-Cars to cover the target and one of them to look for any sign of the return of the inhabitants of Camp A. He then ordered an airstrike on Camp B.

Complying immediately, Red Section's Hunters and a Vampire of Venom Section struck Camp B with Red 1 and 2 attacking two anti-aircraft guns. The pilots reported seeing few people and although light resistance was encountered, the Vampire's drop tank was hit. The leading Vampire aborted its attack due to radio failure. At 0927hrs the refuelled K-Cars were on station and K-Car K2A was sent to cover Camp A to "keep the show going".

The sweeplines closed in on the two camps. A K-Car pilot reported at 0940 hrs that he had in front of him a potential prisoner with his hands up. The records do not say what the outcome was.

As his Lynx orbited the battlefield, Graham had much to do. He warned Jackson's Stop 2 to be wary because MacKenzie's Stop 4 was firing at insurgents in their direction. At 0946hrs he had K-Car K3 attempt to block the escape of cadres in the gap between Stops 1 and 2. Next he had K3 cover Wilson's Stop 6 as they started to search Camp C.

At 0954hrs Lynx D4, flying well north of Camp A, spotted a group of men and was fired on from the nearby road. The

---

[57] BECM RAAP, Box 844, Op *Dingo*, radio message, 26 November 1977.

A Dakota on its way to the Tembué admin area.
Photo: A Pride of Eagles

significance of this find was not realized until the mid-afternoon. Walls's next situation report to ComOps stated that Stops 1 and 2 were "clearing toward B and C. Will clear through to riverline. Numerous trenches and bunkers in B and C which could contain CTs [communist terrorists]. Stop 3 has moved south toward north end of B. Stop 6 will move to road running through C and hold. Stops 1, 2 and 3 are engaging CTs who are attempting to break from the area. Stops 4 and 5 are holding on west bank of river engaging CTs as they flee".[58]

At 1007hrs it was reported that there were many pits in Camp B filled with people. One insurgent was killed in Camp C and an African woman captured by Stop 6 during their search of it. Robinson informed Graham that the SB team would be sent to Camp C once it was secured.

Henson and his Stops 1 and 2 had moved into positions around Camp B while Ken Roberts's Stop 5 remained in a blocking position in the west. Briefing Robinson on this, Graham warned that K2A had drawn fire in the area of the rifle range near Camp A from a small camp equipped with an underground bunker.

Major Henson recalls that, having been ordered "to sweep forward to the river which was about a kilometre away, we came across limited opposition on the way, save that a lot of enemy had climbed into trees to escape the Golf bombs and K-Cars and we were being constantly sniped at. Anyway we eventually arrived at a large camp made of thatched huts alongside the riverbank. I had next to me Corporal Russell Phillips; my thinking was that he had enough courage for both of us and I wasn't feeling particularly brave that day anyway".[59]

At 1015hrs Stop 1 was exchanging shots with ZANLA personnel entrenched on the southern side of Camp B, 400 metres from its centre.

1016–1145hrs

At 1016hrs Walsh and Robinson were back in command. Jackson's Stop 2 had reached the middle of Camp B. Henson with Webb's Stop 1 intended to advance there once they had snuffed out the resistance they faced. Jackson moved his men to the northwest of the camp to avoid the line of fire.

The SB team flew into Camp C at 1019hrs. At Camp B, Stop 1 was still in contact with ZANLA elements. Robinson, however, had to warn Jackson's Stop 2 to move further out of the line of fire because Stop 1 was swinging round toward them.

Camp A had not yet been cleared so he ordered Roberts's Stop 5 to move to a landing zone to be flown to it by helicopter.

K3 was dealing with the small camp near the rifle range. He destroyed all the bunkers except one and silenced all resistance. He reported to Robinson at 1022hrs that the bunker was too deep for his 20mm to penetrate. He added six minutes later that the camp seemed to have a large weapons cache. He suggested two sticks be flown there to examine it. Robinson responded by sending Stop 5 there and MacKenzie's Stop 4 to Camp A.

Because Webb's Stop 1 was still in action in Camp B at 1032hrs, Robinson asked for a K-Car to support them. K2 promptly called in Hunters to attack a 20-man group in the eastern area of Camp B. The pair of Hunters responding fired 18 Matra rockets and 120 30mm cannon shells.

At 1115hrs Mike Webb's Stop 1 had secured Camp B. Henson reported that Stop 1 had killed 25 insurgents in the course of their attack and Jackson's Stop 2 45. They had found only a few bodies in Camp B itself. This was no surprise because the Canberras' initial Alpha bomb strike had overshot most of it.

Robinson reported to General Walls at 1120hrs that Camp C appeared to be a FPLM base. Stops 1 and 2 were starting a detailed search of Camp B. Stop 5 was examining the small camp and its arms cache at the rifle range. They had captured two insurgents who would be flown to the forward admin area for interrogation. Stop 4 would be moved to clear Camp A with the assistance of a Stop 5 stick once the range area was cleared. Stops 1 and 2 had killed 70 and Stop 6 23 insurgents.

At 1123hrs the SB team had finished examining Camp C which Grahame Wilson concluded was an FPLM control centre. He reported he had one prisoner.

The SB team wanted to move to Camp B but Stop 1 was still searching its west side and estimated they needed another 15 minutes. Robinson responded by ordering Willis to move his Stop 3 south from their blocking position. Wilson ordered another search of Camp C and informed Robinson at 1130hrs that all

---

[58] BECM RAAP, Box 844, Op Dingo, radio message, 26 November 1977.

[59] email from Nigel Henson, 27 May 2009.

that was left to do was to burn the huts. The SB men were still with Wilson, waiting for Camp B to be cleared. Robinson ordered Jackson not to set fire to any huts until the SB team had examined them.

Henson interjected to say there was only clothing in the huts. He proposed to collect any documents.

Robinson by then was concentrating on Camp A, having ordered MacKenzie to begin his sweep. MacKenzie reported that one of his men had missed the helicopter lift to Camp A but the records do not betray who he was or what happened to him.

At 1143hrs, Ken Roberts radioed Robinson that his Stop 5 had found the arms cache and begun to open it, finding mortar bombs and weapons.

1145–1245hrs

By 1145hrs Zulu 2 was entering its final phase. Robinson ordered Wilson to leave a stick to protect the SB members and have his men return to their dropping zone to recover their parachutes. Henson then reported the finding of interesting documents by Stop 1 and Robinson sent the SB across to him. As he did, Stop 1 found a cache of weapons.

While waiting for the SB, Major Henson recalls sitting with Corporal Phillips in the shade of "a fairly large thickly vegetated tamarind-type tree when suddenly Phillips yelled out, 'Watch out, sir!' and began revving [shooting] the foliage with his MAG. Well, eventually out tumbled from above my head a number of ZANLA in various degrees of lifelessness and who landed at my feet. Of course, I immediately awarded Russell Phillips every medal I could think of, while at the same time reprimanding him for waking an officer unnecessarily". In the event, Phillips for this and a previous action in a single-handed fight in a cave on 29 September 1977 would be awarded in 1978 the rare Silver Cross of Rhodesia.[60]

Henson then reported that the documents his men had found indicated there was a magazine in the area between Camps B and C. He asked that captured ZANLA prisoners be brought in to indicate its whereabouts. As his Stop 1 was still exchanging fire with the enemy, Webb asked for support from a K-Car and for a new FN rifle and water. Walsh ordered K3A to provide cover for Webb. G-Car Pink 2 delivered the water, the spare rifle, demolition explosives and two prisoners to assist in finding Camp B's magazine.

Because Walsh indicated that the command G-Car needed refuelling, Robinson decided to transfer to a K-Car as Major Mick Graham's Lynx was at Mount Darwin, also refuelling.

While Robinson was doing this, Roberts reported that Stop 5 had emptied the bunker at the camp near the rifle range. They had found a 75mm recoilless rifle, an 82mm mortar, grenades and a large quantity of ammunition. Roberts asked for a demolition kit.

At 1210hrs the aerial reconnaissance by the Lynxes had established that the airstrikes had set fire to five long buildings

[60] email from Nigel Henson, 27 May 2009.

Dropping supplies into the admin area.
Photos: A Pride of Eagles

and surrounding huts at Camp B, and destroyed two 12.7mm machine-gun positions. The complex of huts north of Camp C was burning.

There had been no firing from Tembué village at reconnaissance aircraft. No vehicles had been seen moving from there. One civilian truck had been seen going to Bene and six people climbed out of it.

No other vehicles were seen on the Bene road. Two large ten-tonne trucks were seen heading west some 30 kilometres northwest of Tembué.

Bene airfield was deemed unserviceable due to overgrown grass but Tembué airfield was serviceable.[61]

Back on the scene at 1215hrs, Robinson reported to Walls that the search of Camp C was completed. Stops 1 and 2 were searching Camp B and found numerous interesting documents and weapons. They had found the radio hut but no radio. They were still having intermittent contacts.

At Camp A, MacKenzie and his Stop 4 were in action. A rock rolling down the side of a *donga* alerted MacKenzie to six ZANLA cadres hiding in a cave. Before they could fire their SKS rifles, MacKenzie killed them all with rapid bursts from his 5.5mm AR-15 rifle. Shortly after, MacKenzie, Sergeant Les Clark and Trooper Gerry McGowan, an RPD gunner, flushed a large group out of another *donga*, killing 86 of them.[62]

Elsewhere, the other stops were occupied with more mundane tasks. Wilson's Stop 6 was collecting parachutes.

Webb of Stop 1 had asked for more water and ammunition. Robinson responded by asking any incoming G-Car to carry water for his thirsty troops.

Webb alerted Robinson to the sound of a heavy weapon firing in the north. Robinson asked MacKenzie if he needed support. MacKenzie replied he needed K-Car support. Willis explained the firing heard in his area was at ZANLA cadres who had run into his stop line.

The weather intruded, leading Robinson to ask MacKenzie at 1230hrs whether he would still require K-Car support given the approaching storms. MacKenzie replied: "Not required at this time."

At 1241hrs Henson reported to Robinson that the main portion of Camp B had been cleared.

Nigel Henson remembers: "After we had searched the camp, we were told to turn right and move north along the right bank of the river which we did. The river at this point was about 150 metres wide and was a sea of reeds and bullrushes. We moved along for another km or so, killing many hiding ZANLA—a lot in the camp latrines and further trees— and eventually arrived at a large 82mm mortar pit."

Robinson then ordered Willis's Stop 3 to sweep the area southward to Camp B where, he added to Henson, Stop 1 would wait for Stop 3 to join them. Both would then clear the area back to the dropping zone to collect their parachutes. Henson replied that they had found an 82mm mortar. He proposed that it should be flown out.

In the event, Henson recalls: "We then destroyed this weapon plus numerous other small arms we had collected. At this stage we had not seen any other Rhodesian troops but we were told to return to our DZ and begin collecting parachutes. This we did. The SAS under Colin Willis then swept the river in a southerly direction when we were out of the way. We came in for a fair amount of criticism as we had not swept the river—we were instructed to keep out of it—where the SAS subsequently killed a lot of ZANLA hiding in the reeds."[63]

At 1245hrs Robinson briefed Major Mick Graham who was flying in to relieve him. He explained that Stop 4 was searching Camp A from south to north. Stop 5 was clearing the camp near the range. Stops 1 and 2 had searched Camp B. Stop 3 was moving down to join 1 and 2. Stop 6 was collecting parachutes.

---

[61] BECM RAAP, Box 844, Op *Dingo*, sitrep, A4/F4/9A, 26 November 1977.

[62] BECM RAAP, Box 844, Op *Dingo*, radio message, 26 November 1977; Cole, p. 188.

[63] email from Nigel Henson, 27 May 2009.

A Lynx overflies the Dingo 2 operational area.
Photo: A Pride of Eagles

1245–1354hrs

At 1250hrs Red Section replaced the top cover. Below them Stops 1 and 2 were awaiting the arrival of Stop 3 before moving off to collect parachutes which Stop 6 was already doing. Stop 4 was searching Camp A. Stop 5 had cleared the rifle range and was waiting for the arrival of their requested demolition kits for the weapons they had collected. A storm was approaching from the north and it was already raining.

MacKenzie's clearing of Camp A was interrupted briefly when he found at 1315hrs that its southern portion had been re-occupied by ZANLA. He called for air support but the rain inhibited the K-Cars from responding. Instead he had to make do with a Lynx reconnaissance of the southern portion. When, however, he ordered an advance of his Stop 4, any ZANLA resistance melted away. He reported to Mick Graham that his men had found 20 British SLR [the British version of the FN) among 100 SKS rifles. At 1325hrs he asked Graham for the SB team to be flown to him to examine the camp's office. They arrived promptly in G-Car Pink 4.

G-Car Yellow 2 delivered the ammunition and water requested by Stop 1 and collected from them the demolition explosives requested by Roberts, waiting at rifle range camp. Graham ordered Jackson's Stop 2 to collect the recovered parachutes and preparations began for their removal by G-Car. When Robinson returned at 1354hrs, Graham told him that Stops 1–3 were in B Camp and would meet the G-Cars in the landing zone.

1354–1449hrs

As Robinson resumed command, Stop 5 started blowing up eight boxes of 82mm mortar rounds, eight boxes of RGD and two of concussion grenades, 15 boxes of 7.62mm intermediate bullets, eight 75mm recoilless rounds, two TMH anti-tank mines, four boxes of TNT, four boxes of 7.62mm long ammunition and 15 SKS rifles.

MacKenzie reported Camp A was clear and that the SB members were examining the headquarters block and would need an hour to do so. He began the demolition of 140 SKS rifles, 20 British SLR rifles, a 12.7mm DshK heavy machine gun, 30 rifle grenades, 10,000 7.62mm intermediate rounds, 15 slabs of TNT, one 3.5in rocket launcher, an 82mm mortar, a 4.5 truck, 1,000 sets of denims and ten tons of maize. He and his men had killed 150 of the inhabitants of Camp A.

At 1400hrs the cab-rank was cancelled because of the weather. As Red Section's Hunters, the latest flying in the cab-rank, had withdrawn at 1330hrs and for the rest of the day the fighter aircraft remained on standby at New Sarum. Robinson requested six G-Cars to begin to fly out all the stop groups except for MacKenzie's. K-Car K1A offered to fly out three of the 12.7mm machine guns found at Camp B, if they were dismantled. Henson had Jackson dismantle them. Unusually two of these weapons had been mounted on mounds and not dug-in positions. Both guns were found loaded and cocked but their crews had fled. The third gun was on open ground, lying on its side.

While the rest of Stop 3 collected parachutes, Willis and a couple of his men blew up the remaining arms and ammunition of Camp B's armoury. They destroyed three 75mm recoilless rifles and 25 of their 75mm shells, two 82mm mortars, 15 TMH and an unopened crate of anti-tank landmines, five boxes of TNT, two of grenades, a 3.5in rocket launcher and six SKS rifles.

At 1420hrs, Robinson reported to General Walls that he estimated the total kill at 300–350.

Six G-Cars flew Stop 1 from Camp B to the landing zone to gather the parachutes. The SB team had completed their examination and were flown out of Camp A by G-Car Pink 4 along with documents and two captives who turned out to be Rhodesian Internal Affairs district assistants who had been abducted by ZANLA on 21 November. They had been marched across the border and then taken by vehicle to be imprisoned in Tembué.

With regard to the order of the withdrawal of units, the command Dakota signalled that Jackson's Stop 2 would be the first unit to be flown out. Stop 2 had just seen two red trucks driving on a nearby road but was told to ignore them. Willis's team still needed another half an hour to complete their demolition in Camp B. This was done by 1448hrs, so Willis signalled they were ready for uplift. They were flown to join the rest of Stop 3 collecting parachutes along the landing zone.

1449hrs–0515hrs

MacKenzie contacted Walsh and Robinson to give them the news that he had discovered why the camps had been emptier than expected. A captured man had told him that 1,000 men had left during the previous night for another camp some distance to the north. Another group of 500 had gone south to Bene. Walsh responded by despatching a Lynx to conduct a search to the north.

MacKenzie's Stop 4 was still clearing Camp A and because they were still encountering insurgents, MacKenzie asked for K-Car cover. This was provided and by 1500hrs, the K-Car was drawing fire.

At 1530hrs, with most of his men still gathering up their parachutes and Stop 4 still embroiled in Camp A, Robinson radioed Walls a warning that it might not be possible to withdraw all the men that afternoon. The command Dakota was leaving to refuel so Robinson gave Walls the latest estimate which was 350 ZANLA dead. In addition, caches of heavy weapons, small arms and munitions had been destroyed.

Walsh had to leave at 1538hrs to refuel from the forward admin area. On the short journey to the refuelling point, Robinson and Walls decided that Stops 1, 2 and 6 would be flown out together with all the parachutes and jump helmets. Stops 3 and 5 would spend the night in Camp B and Stop 6 in Camp A. Walls also concluded that, because of the few hours of daylight left and the stormy weather the command Dakota would not return from Mount Darwin. Instead he intended to monitor the last stages from Mount Darwin.

Half an hour earlier, Walsh had reported the finding of the fourth camp by the Lynx. It was 15.3 kilometres north of Camp A. Permission was promptly given by Walls for it to be bombed. By 1527hrs it was known to comprise newly constructed huts under trees and a parade ground. Lynx C4 was ordered to mark it for an airstrike by Hunters followed by Canberras, bombing with Alpha bombs.

This was duly done at 1615hrs. Striking the penultimate blow of the day, C4 fired his smoke rocket. Blue Section's Hunters dived in, firing 64 Matra rockets into the camp, marking it for the closely following Canberras, tucked down at 300 feet. The 1,200 Alpha bombs bounded forward and exploded among the huts, setting half of them on fire. Blue Section wheeled round and came in again and ran 700 30mm shells through the camp. The Hunters and Canberras flew back to New Sarum where the Canberra aircrews stood down at 1820hrs.

Nigel Henson, Mike Webb and his Stop 1 were lifted from the target area and flown to the forward admin area to guard it for the night. Stops 2 and 6 left in twelve helicopters, bound for 'The Train', Chiswiti and ultimately Mount Darwin.

Willis's Stop 3 at Camp C, Roberts's Stop 5 at Camp B and MacKenzie's Stop 4 at Camp A adopted all-round defence and settled down to another night in Mozambique.

The journey home for the K-Cars and G-Cars was not without drama. The line of storms meant they did not all reach Mount Darwin as planned. One Alouette ran out of fuel short of 'The Train' and had to land on an island on Lake Cabora Bassa to await a delivery of four drums of fuel by parachute from Malloch's DC-7. After refuelling, it was escorted over the Rhodesian border by other helicopters. The growing darkness, the rain and the turbulence led to the dispersal of the helicopters. The first wave, en route to Mount Darwin, made an unplanned stop at the Centenary Country Club. The second wave, including Walsh and Robinson in the command helicopter and Stops 2 and 6, landed at Chiswiti.[64]

It was the end of another long day. Squadron Leader Griffiths, for example, had flown K-Car K1 for eight hours and thirty-five minutes.[65]

The striking of the final blow of the day, however, fell to the FPLM. At 1805hrs the BSAP post at Kanyemba reported that a DC-4 aircraft had been hit by a missile while flying north over the Zambian–Mozambican border between Feira and Zumbo at the Zambezi–Luangwa river confluence. The aircraft, one of Rhodesia's sanctions-breakers owned by Jack Malloch, was carrying ten tons of fresh prime beef for export. The aircraft turned south and crash-landed just over the southern bank of the Zambezi River close to the Rhodesian border. The event was confirmed by the FPLM report from Zumbo at 0740hrs the next day. It admitted responsibility for firing the missile and related that the aircraft had been found and its crew—two white men, Captain Mouzon and First Lieutenant Nibel—had been captured.[66]

The last order of the day granted Jackson's Stop 2 a day off duty to refit before they returned to the operational area.[67] This was extended to all the troops on the next day.[68] The night for the men left at Tembué was hardly restful as they listened to heavy vehicles moving and distant bursts of heavy machine-gun fire. Stop 5's sentries in Camp B were busy shooting at stragglers and MacKenzie had to retake Camp A at dawn, killing more ZANLA and rescuing a prisoner, an abducted African Selous Scout.

0515–1310hrs

At 0515hrs aircraft of the Rhodesian Air Force were airborne, heading back to Tembué to provide cover for the three SAS stop groups still there. The first there at 0711hrs was Lynx E4 carrying Major Mick Graham, drawing fire from a KPV 14.5mm anti-aircraft gun and a multi-barrelled gun positioned on the road south of the camps.

At 0625hrs all the G-Cars had been assembled at Chiswiti and were leaving in sections. The first four G-Cars, A Section, were expected at Tembué at 0945hrs to pick up 24 parachutes and eight men from Stop 5. B Section would land at the forward admin area to fly out twelve men from Stop 1. It was estimated that the withdrawal could be effected by 40 helicopter lifts using the 22 available G-Cars. At 0820hrs Graham informed all stops that the command Dakota and Robinson were en route and would take over command. Five minutes later, Graham warned the command Dakota and the helicopters to be wary of flying over known anti-aircraft positions west of Bene.

At 0900hrs the Hunters orbited the camps. Half an hour later, K-Cars K2 and K2A escorted in the G-Cars.

At New Sarum the evident lack of enemy threat to the

---

[64] Cole, p. 188.

[65] Flying log of H.G. Griffiths, Vol. 4.

[66] BECM RAAP, Box 844, Op Dingo, radio message, 26 November 1977, B2, 27 November 1977.

[67] BECM RAAP, Box 844, Op Dingo, telex, 26 November 1977.

[68] BECM RAAP, Box 844, Op Dingo, telex, 27 November 1977.

withdrawal led to one Canberra having its six 1,000lb bombs unloaded. The other three remained on standby, two with loads of 300 Alpha bombs and one with six 500lb bombs. The helicopter shuttle by 1052hrs left behind only the forward area personnel and MacKenzie's Stop 4 who had not had time to recover their parachutes, 20 of which were draped in the trees. His men had all been lifted out by 1218hrs and at 1310hrs the final six G-Cars took off from the forward administration area, carrying 20 men, including prisoners.

Thereafter the personnel on 'The Train' were flown out. Graeme Murdoch and his stick were the last to leave the forward admin area, flying in Nick Meikle's G-Car. He took them back to New Sarum and then drove them in his own car to the gates of the RLI barracks, ending Operation *Dingo*.

CHAPTER ELEVEN:
THE THIRD BLOW: OPERATION VIRILE, 27–30 NOVEMBER 1977

Rhodesia's strike aircraft could now be released to support Operation *Virile*, the bridge-blowing exercise designed to inhibit the movement of ZANLA toward Rhodesia's eastern border.

At last light on 27 November 1977, *Virile* was underway. Major Albert Sachse's Selous Scouts' vehicles drove over the Mozambican border on a little-used track just east of Espungabera, heading for the main road to the small town of Dombe. The first bridge was blown to isolate Espungabera before the column headed northeast to Dombe, led by the unique Pookie landmine-detection vehicle. When the Pookie broke down on the rugged road, it was replaced in the lead by an innocent-looking 'Q' armoured bus with a concealed armament of a DShK 12.7mm and two Browning .5in heavy machine guns and carrying 'passengers' armed with RPD machine guns.

A narrow shave in a FPLM ambush, however, led to the bus being replaced at the head of the column by two less vulnerable armoured cars, armed with 20mm Hispano cannons. In addition, the road was cleared ahead by two Hunters strafing vehicles. The Hunters attacked Dombe to discourage FPLM interference while the Scouts demolished the high-level, four-spanned bridge over the Mabvudzi River.

The column turned back to blow the six-span bridge over the Lusito River at 0900hrs on Monday, 28 November. The next attack, on a sawmill, however, annoyed the South African Government because, during it, the Selous Scouts directed a Hunter attack onto what they mistook for a gun emplacement and destroyed the main radio relay station for the Cabora Bassa–Transvaal, South Africa power line.

On Tuesday, 29 November, the Scouts blew up two more bridges and abandoned heavy road-making machinery. At dusk they returned to the Espungabera area and crossed back into Rhodesia at 1000hrs on Wednesday morning, 30 November, leaving Espungabera cut off from the northeast by fast-flowing rivers. Ambush parties thereafter harassed the portering of supplies between the destroyed bridges, calling down Hunter attacks on FPLM vehicles bringing supplies to the river crossings. What surprised the ambushers was the unpopularity of the governing FRELIMO among the local Mozambicans they met. This encouraged the Rhodesian Government to support the resistance movement which came to be known as RENAMO.[69]

---

[69] Reid-Daly, *Top Secret War*, pp. 285–296.

Vehicles of a rampaging Selous Scouts' flying column.
Photo: The Saints

Top, above left and facing page: Elements of 2 Commando combined with Selous Scouts on this raid. Pictured in this series are the vehicles of the rampant 'flying column'—one of the Scouts' favourite and ruthlessly successful modus operandi when striking at ZANLA.
Photo: The Saints

Above right: Captured terrorist.
Photo: The Saints

CHAPTER TWELVE:
THE CONSEQUENCES

On Monday, 28 November, ComOps issued a brief communiqué which said nothing more than that, in the past five days, Rhodesian forces had attacked camps near Chimoio and Tembué, killing more than 1,200 ZANLA.[70] The unofficial estimate was that ZANLA had suffered some 5,000 casualties. It was calculated that ZANLA had suffered a loss of 20 per cent of its strength in the two raids.[71]

Given their experience of being the target of the hostility of the international press since before UDI in 1965, the Rhodesians should not have been surprised by what the British press in particular reported. Derek Ingram of the Gemini News Service had been in Chimoio town on the morning of 23 November and had heard the explosions and had seen the smoke rising on the northern horizon. He was only able to visit the camp after the last troops left but would report seeing the bodies of nearly 100 young teenagers being buried. Ian Christie, another British journalist, joined him, counting the remains of 20 young teenage girls in one grave. Christie noted that the 70 other corpses strewn about were mostly female and many of them children. At the Parirenyatwa Camp hospital, which had burned down, eight men lay under a tree, all shot through the back of the head. A napalm attack had burned children between 8 and 14 years old at Chindunduma Primary School. Later there were photographs published of mass graves with bodies piled in layers.[72]

To counter this depiction of *Dingo* as a massacre of the unarmed and the innocent, ComOps spokesmen, including General Walls,

---

[70] Legum, p. B342.

[71] McAleese, p. 142; Papers in private hands (PPH), Ops 001, debrief Op *Dingo* Phase 2 (Z2), 28 November 1977.

[72] Caute, pp. 140–141.

conceded that there had been unarmed ZANLA personnel killed. They maintained nevertheless that most of those killed had been armed. They spoke in praise of a courageous group who, armed with folding-butt FN rifles, had resisted fiercely when cornered. The point at issue, the Rhodesians insisted, was that the camps were full of future infiltrators and that the camps could not just be allowed to exist.

General Walls warned that his forces would continue to operate externally. He added that, if women inhabited the camps, they could be killed.[73]

The Rhodesians were surprised when Britain's Foreign Secretary, Dr David Owen, struck a different note. He deplored *Dingo* as a "savage and pretty brutal attack" which had endangered the peace of the whole of southern Africa. He added, however, it might have proved to Mugabe and Nkomo and their Patriotic Front "that the Rhodesian Defence Force is not on its back".[74]

In the aftermath of *Dingo*, a revolt within ZANU/ZANLA over the conduct of the war led to the arrest and incarceration of Cleotus Chigowe after he had abducted Mugabe's close colleagues, Edgar Tekere and Dr Herbert Ushewokunze.[75]

On 3 March 1978 Ian Smith achieved a settlement with the internal nationalists that held the potential of defeating Mugabe and Nkomo. He was well on the road to that settlement before the attack on Tembué because on Friday, 25 November, the Reverend Ndabaningi Sithole (who had founded ZANU in 1963 only to be ousted by Mugabe in 1974) welcomed Smith's invitation to talk. Senator Chief Jeremiah Chirau, president of the Zimbabwe United People's Organization, did likewise on Sunday, 27 November. The key player, however, was Bishop Muzorewa.

Although on 26 November he praised Smith's commitment to majority rule, within three days he was responding to the outrage of his constituents and refusing to negotiate with Smith because of the killing of his kinsmen at Chimoio and Tembué. It took a few weeks before Muzorewa was prepared to negotiate.

Given a large slice of luck, Operation *Dingo* had been a stunning technical and political success. It had harassed ZANLA in its safe havens, killed or wounded 20 per cent of its strength, and set back the reinforcement effort by months. The Rhodesian intelligence services gleaned much from the vast quantity of documents recovered. Lessons had been learned that improvisation could counter the short range of the Alouette III and other disadvantages. The experiment of using a command helicopter taught that a more capable aircraft was needed. More flexible tactics on the ground with regard to the sweeplines were acknowledged as necessary. The new A76 radios were praised but were found to be likely to fail if wet. Difficult-to-obtain weapons had been captured but it was apparent that, if heavy weapons like the 37mm anti-aircraft gun were to be recovered, larger and more powerful helicopters were required.[76] A year later the Rhodesian Air Force acquired Agusta-Bell 206s with greater range and lifting capacity.

Many more airborne and other raids followed. If the enemy became wary, and success on a *Dingo* scale was never repeated, Rhodesia's external operations convinced her neighbours that the war had to end.

The raids forced Mugabe and Nkomo to the conference table in September 1979 to accept the compromise devised by Lord Carrington and the British Foreign and Commonwealth Office at Lancaster House, London, that December. The ironic product was the accession to power of Robert Mugabe in the subsequent election in early 1980 and what happened thereafter.

---

[73] Cole, pp. 188–189.

[74] Flower, pp. 191–193; *Keesing's*, 28 April 1978, Vol. XXIV, p. 28948.

[75] Cole, p. 189; Tekere, p. 98.

[76] PPH, Ops 001, debrief Op Dingo Phase 2 (Z2), 28 November 1977.

*To Carole, Andy, Carrie-Ann
and now Michaela
who make everything possible*

I owe the chance to write this book to the dynamic team of Chris and Kerrin Cocks of 30° South Publishers. Much of it is based on the papers lodged in the British Empire and Commonwealth Museum, Bristol, England and on the memoirs and comments from the veterans of *Dingo*. Some of it is drawn from my study of Fireforce when second-in-command of the Research Section of the Rhodesian Intelligence Corps.

Operation *Dingo* was an extraordinary joint services' operation. I have found, when lecturing on it to professional military audiences, utter disbelief that such a double blow could be struck so far into hostile territory by less than 200 troops and a collection of aircraft that, by 1977, should have been gracing someone's museum.

Dr Richard Wood, BA (Hons) (Rhodes), PhD (Edinburgh), FRHistS, was born in Bulawayo, Zimbabwe. He was educated at St George's College in Harare (then Salisbury), Rhodes University in Grahamstown, South Africa, and Edinburgh University, Scotland. He was a Commonwealth scholar and is a Fellow of the Royal Historical Society. He was the Ernest Oppenheimer Memorial Research Fellow at the University of Rhodesia and a Professor of History at the University of Durban-Westville, South Africa. He is undoubtedly the foremost historian and researcher on the history of Rhodesia in the decades following World War II and, with exclusive access to the hitherto closed papers of Ian Smith, has written three definitive publications and is currently working on the final volume in the series that will cover the period 1970–1980. He is a renowned military historian, having served as a territorial soldier in the 1st and 8th Battalions, the Rhodesia Regiment, and in the Mapping and Research Unit of the Rhodesian Intelligence Corps. He has published numerous articles and chapters in books, including in Daniel Marston's and Cart Malkasian's, *Counterinsurgency in Modern Warfare* (Osprey, 2008) and is the author of several books on the history and politics of Rhodesia, as listed at the front of this publication.